THE 2021 WOOD PELLET MASTERY COOKBOOK

2 Books in 1: The New Complete Guide for Perfect Smoking and Grilling | 100+ Quick and Easy Recipes That Your Family Will Love

Table of Contents

Introduction

Pit boss grills and smokers are outdoor charcoal grills and smokers that use flavored wood pellets as fuel. Since it does not need gas or electricity, it is an environmentally friendly cooking alternative. You can enjoy fresh outdoor cooking using your own ingredients with this setup. As a result, it is a better choice because you can monitor the amount of nicotine and preservatives in your meal.

By using high-quality products and producing a product with a large brewing power, the business has gained a good reputation. Smoking any form of food is simple with a Pit Boss grill. Small, medium, and high temperatures are among the choices for smoking temperature provided by the company. Various models for smoking with various wood pellets or smoking methods are available. These are perfect for beginners who need to warm up before beginning a meal, as well as seasoned chefs who want to try out new meat flavors.

This Pit Boss Pellet Grill Review will give you a thorough understanding of the grill's key features. You'll find that it has a sleek design and a stylish exterior that makes it both attractive and practical. It's also transportable. As previously mentioned, you can use electricity or wood pellets to power this grill, and its high-quality construction ensures its longevity.

You'll also be able to enjoy every feature because this smoker is made of professional-grade materials, ensuring long-term use. It can handle a wide range of foods, including delicate things such as fish and meat. This grill will appeal to any taste while keeping the food safe.

Pit Boss Grills are made with multiple vents to provide cooking space even under a heavy load. They feature a non-stick finish for easy cleaning and a stainless steel drip pan to catch the grease that makes it through the grate. Our grills are ready for whatever you're going to throw at them! Order yours today!

Beef recipes

1. Grilled Veal Shoulder Roast with Fennel and Thyme Rub

Preparation Time: 15 minutes

Cooking Time: 55 minutes

Servings: 8

Ingredients

- 3 1/2 lb boneless veal shoulder roast

- 2 tablespoon dried thyme leaves

- 1 fresh fennel, thinly sliced

- 2 tablespoon fresh thyme, chopped

- 3/4 teaspoon kosher salt and ground white pepper

- 4 tablespoon olive oil

- 1/2 cup white wine

Directions:

1. Place a shoulder roast in a large dish and rub with salt and pepper.

2. In a bowl, combine thyme, fennel, salt and pepper, wine and oil.

3. Rub the meat generously.

4. Start your Pit Boss grill, set the temperature on High and preheat, lid closed, for 10 to 15 minutes.

5. Grill about 25 minutes at high temperatures or to your preference for doneness.

6. Remove the veal chops from the grill. Take their temperature with your meat thermometer. The veal chops

should have a temperature of 130 degrees Fahrenheit for medium-rare or 140 degrees for medium.

7.   Serve hot.

Nutrition:

Calories 322.71

Fat 12.14g

Carbohydrates 4.64g

Fiber 1.39g

Protein 36.23g

2. Grilled Veal with Mustard Lemony Crust
Preparation Time: 15 minutes

Cooking Time: 2 hours and 45 minutes

Servings: 8

Ingredients

- 1 lb boneless veal leg round roast

- 1 tablespoon Dijon-style mustard

- 1 tablespoon lemon juice

- 1 teaspoon dried thyme, crushed

- 1 teaspoon dried basil, crushed

- 2 tablespoon water

- 1/2 teaspoon coarsely salt and ground pepper

- 1/4 cup breadcrumbs

Directions:

1. Place meat on a rack in a shallow roasting pan.

2. In a small mixing bowl stir together bread crumbs, water, mustard, lemon juice, basil, thyme, and pepper. Spread the mixture over surface of the meat.

3. Start your Pit Boss grill, set the temperature on High and preheat, lid closed, for 10 to 15 minutes.

4. As a general rule, you should grill steaks on high heat (450-500°F).

5. Grill about 7-10 minutes per side at high temperatures or 15-20 minutes per side at the lower temperatures, or to your preference for doneness.

6. Remove veal meat from the grill and let cool for 10 minutes.

Nutrition:

Calories 172 cal

Fat 3g

Carbohydrates 4g

Fiber 0g

Protein 30g

3. Beef Tenderloin with Balsamic Glaze

Preparation Time: 30 minutes

Cooking Time: 10 minutes

Servings: 6

Ingredients

- Balsamic Reduction

- 3-4 tablespoons of butter

- 1/3 cups of brown sugar

- 3 tablespoons of fresh rosemary finely chopped

- 3 cups of balsamic vinegar

- 3 garlic cloves of peeled and crushed

- Salt and pepper

- Beef Tenderloin

- Remove silver skin from the trimmed meat

Directions:

1. Cook the tail (chain portion) by folding it up to ensure an even grilling. Old, the tail together with toothpicks or a butcher's twine, then season with beef rub.

2. Pre-heat wooden Pit Boss smoker grill to about 250 degrees F. At the bottom of the rack, cook the meat for about sixty minutes. Keep an eye on the loins. Let the tender loins reach an average temperature of 115 degrees.

3. Extract the meat from the grill and let cool off. The next thing is to increase the grill heat to about 500 degrees F to sear. Once this is done, place the meat on the searing rack and sear each side for about a minute.

4. The final temperature of the dish should be about 130 degrees. Extract tenderloin from the grill and allow cooling off on a cutting board. With a sharp chef knife, slice the meat into strips. Take the balsamic reduction and drizzle over meat to get the final product.

Nutrition:

Calories: 40 cal

Carbohydrates: 0g

Fat: 3g

Protein: 8g

Fiber: 0g

4. Chipotle Rubbed Tri-Tip

Preparation Time: 30 minutes

Cooking Time: 30 minutes

Servings: 4-6

Ingredients

- 1 beef tri-tip

- Extra virgin olive oil

- Your favorite salsa, for serving

For the rub:

- 1 tablespoon coarse salt (kosher or sea)

- 1-1/2 teaspoons Chipotle chili powder

- 1-1/2 teaspoons Oregano, preferably Mexican

- 1 teaspoon granulated garlic

- 1/2 teaspoon ground cumin

- 1/2 teaspoon freshly ground black pepper

Directions:

1. Fire up your Pit Boss grill to medium-high, preferably at about 225 degrees.

2. You could opt for mesquite or your favorite flavor of Pit Bosss.

3. Mix ingredients to make the rub in a small clean bowl, stir until it is well combined.

4. Ensure your hands are clean. Next, place the tri-tip in a baking dish and sprinkle rub all over the sides, using your fingers, pat the rub into the meat. Drizzle some amount of virgin olive oil over mixture and rub.

5. Next, transfer the tri-tip to the grill. Reduce the lid and grill the tri-tip until the grill heats up to 100 degrees. Grill for about one hour. Sometimes, it could take lesser time. Remove tri-tip from grill and place in a plate with a foil covering.

6. Heat grill again till about 600 degrees. When at 600 degrees, switch to Open Flame Cooking Mode. Carefully pull out the grill grates and the Hatch and replace with the Direct Flame Insert.

7. Extract the tri-tip from the foil. Place on sear. Sear the tri-tip until it reaches about 120 degrees. It would be crusty and browned on the outside and rare in the center; 130 degrees for medium-rare (or to taste). Cook the two sides for about 4 minutes, turning with thongs. Transfer the tri-tip to a board and cut.

8. Cool meat for about 2 minutes. With a knife make thin cuts across the grain. Top with your favorite salsa and enjoy.

Nutrition:

Calories: 50 cal

Carbohydrates: 4g

Fat: 8g

Protein: 7.6g

Fiber: 3.2g

5. Bacon-Swiss Cheesesteak Meatloaf
Preparation Time: 15 minutes

Cooking Time: 2 hours

Servings: 8-10

Ingredients:

- 1 tablespoon canola oil

- 2 garlic cloves, finely chopped

- 1 medium onion, finely chopped

- 1 poblano chile, stemmed, seeded, and finely chopped

- 2 pounds extra-lean ground beef

- 2 tablespoons Montreal steak seasoning

- 1 tablespoon A.1. Steak Sauce

- ½ pound bacon, cooked and crumbled

- 2 cups shredded Swiss cheese

- 1 egg, beaten

- 2 cups breadcrumbs

- ½ cup Tiger Sauce

Directions:

1. On your stove top, heat the canola oil in a medium sauté pan over medium-high heat. Add the garlic, onion, and poblano, and sauté for 3 to 5 minutes, or until the onion is just barely translucent.

2. Supply your smoker with wood pellets and follow the manufacturer's specific start-up

procedure. Preheat, with the lid closed, to 225°F.

3.   In a large bowl, combine the sautéed vegetables, ground beef, steak seasoning, steak sauce, bacon, Swiss cheese, egg, and breadcrumbs. Mix with your hands until well incorporated, then shape into a loaf.

4.   Put the meatloaf in a cast iron skillet and place it on the grill. Insert meat thermometer inserted in the loaf reads 165°F.

5.   Top with the meatloaf with the Tiger Sauce, remove from the grill, and let rest for about 10 minutes before serving.

Nutrition:

Calories: 120 Cal

Fat: 2 g

Carbohydrates: 0 g

Protein: 23 g

Fiber: 0 g

6. London Broil
Preparation Time: 20 minutes

Cooking Time: 12-16 minutes

Servings: 3-4

Ingredients:

- 1 (1½- to 2-pound) London broil or top round steak

- ¼ cup soy sauce

- 2 tablespoons white wine

- 2 tablespoons extra-virgin olive oil

- ¼ cup chopped scallions

- 2 tablespoons packed brown sugar

- 2 garlic cloves, minced

- 2 teaspoons red pepper flakes

- 1 teaspoon freshly ground black pepper

Directions:

1. Using a meat mallet, pound the steak lightly all over on both sides to break down its fibers and tenderize. You are not trying to pound down the thickness.

2. In a medium bowl, make the marinade by combining the soy sauce, white wine, olive oil, scallions, brown sugar, garlic, red pepper flakes, and black pepper.

3. Put the steak in a shallow plastic container with a lid and pour the marinade over the meat. Cover and refrigerate for 4 hours.

4. Supply your smoker with wood pellets and follow the manufacturer's specific start-up procedure. Preheat, with the lid closed, to 350°F.

5. Place the steak directly on the grill, close the lid, and smoke for 6 minutes. Flip, then smoke with the lid closed for 6 to 10 minutes more, or until a meat thermometer inserted in the meat reads 130°F for medium-rare.

6. The meat's temperature will rise by about 5 degrees while it rests.

Nutrition:

Calories: 316 Cal

Fat: 3 g

Carbohydrates: 0 g

Protein: 54 g

Fiber: 0 g

7. Wood Pellet Grilled Bacon

Preparation Time: 30 Minutes

Cooking Time: 25 Minutes

Servings: 6

Ingredients:

- 1 lb. bacon, thickly cut

Directions:

1. Preheat your wood pellet grill to 375°**F.**

2. Line a baking sheet with parchment paper, then place the bacon on it in a single layer.

3. Close the lid and bake for 20 minutes. Flip over, close the top, and bake for an additional 5 minutes.

4. Serve with the favorite side and enjoy it.

Nutrition:

Calories 315

Total fat 14g

Saturated fat 10g

Protein 9g

Sodium: 500mg

8. Wood Pellet Grilled Pork Chops

Preparation Time: 20 Minutes

Cooking Time: 10 Minutes

Servings: 6

Ingredients:

- Six pork chops, thickly cut

- BBQ rub

Directions:

1. Preheat the wood pellet to 450°**F.**

2. Season the pork chops generously with the BBQ rub. Place the pork chops on the grill and cook for 6 minutes or until the internal temperature reaches 145°F.

3. Remove from the grill and let sit for 10 minutes before serving.

4. Enjoy.

Nutrition:

Calories 264

Total fat 13g

Saturated fat 6g

Total Carbs 4g

Net Carbs 1g

Protein 33g

Fiber 3g

Sodium: 66mg

9. Wood Pellet Blackened Pork Chops

Preparation Time: 5 Minutes

Cooking Time: 20 Minutes

Servings: 6

Ingredients:

- Six pork chops

- 1/4 cup blackening seasoning

- Salt and pepper to taste

Directions:

1. Preheat your grill to 375°**F.**

2. Meanwhile, generously season the pork chops with the blackening seasoning, salt, and pepper.

3. Place the pork chops on the grill and close the lid.

4. Let grill for 8 minutes, then flip the chops. Cook until the internal temperature reaches 142°F.

5. Remove the chops from the grill and let rest for 10 minutes before slicing.

6. Serve and enjoy.

Nutrition:

Calories 333

Total fat 18g

Saturated fat 6g

Total Carbs 1g

Protein 40g,

Fiber 1g

Sodium: 3175mg

10. Teriyaki Pineapple Pork Tenderloin Sliders
Preparation Time: 20 Minutes

Cooking Time: 20 Minutes

Servings: 6

Ingredients:

- 1-1/2 lb. pork tenderloin
- One can pineapple ring
- One package king's Hawaiian rolls
- 8 oz teriyaki sauce
- 1-1/2 tbsp salt
- 1 tbsp onion powder
- 1 tbsp paprika
- 1/2 tbsp garlic powder
- 1/2 tbsp cayenne pepper

Directions:

1. Add all the fixings for the rub in a mixing bowl and mix until well mixed. Generously rub the pork loin with the mixture.

2. Heat the pellet to 325°F. Place the meat on a grill and cook while you turn it every 4 minutes.

3. Cook until the internal temperature reaches 145°F.remove from the grill and let it rest for 5 minutes.

4. Meanwhile, open the pineapple can and place the pineapple rings on the grill. Flip the rings when they have a dark brown color.

5. At the same time, half the rolls and place them on the grill and grill them until toasty browned.

6. Assemble the slider by putting the bottom roll first, followed by the pork tenderloin, pineapple ring, a drizzle of sauce, and top with the other roll half. Serve and enjoy.

Nutrition:

Calories 243

Total fat 5g

Saturated fat 2g

Total Carbs 4g

Net Carbs 15g

Protein 33g

Sugar 10g,

Fiber 1g

Sodium: 2447mg

11. Pit Boss Smoked Pulled Lamb Sliders

Preparation Time: 10 Minutes

Cooking Time: 9 Hours

Servings: 7

Ingredients:

- 5 lb. lamb shoulder, boneless

- 1/2 cup olive oil

- 1/3 cup kosher salt

- 1/3 cup pepper, coarsely ground

- 1/3 cup granulated garlic

For the spritz

- 4 oz Worcestershire sauce

- 6 oz apple cider vinegar

Directions:

1. Preheat the Pit Boss to 2250F with a pan of water for moisture.

2. Trim any excess fat from the lamb, then pat it dry with some paper towel. Rub with oil, salt, pepper, and garlic.

3. Place the lamb in the Pit Boss smoker for 90 minutes, then spritz every 30 minutes until the internal temperature reaches 1650F.

4. Transfer the lamb to a foil pan, then add the remaining spritz liquid. Cover with a foil and place back in the Pit Boss.

5. Smoke until the internal temperature reaches 2050F.

6. Remove from the smoker and let rest in a cooler without ice for 30 minutes before pulling it.

7. Serve with slaw or bun and enjoy.

Nutrition:

Calories 235

Total Fat 6g

Total Carbs 22g

Protein 20g

Sugars 7g

Fiber 1g

Sodium 592mg

Potassium 318mg

12. Pit Boss Smoked Lamb Meatballs
Preparation Time: 10 Minutes

Cooking Time: 1 Hour

Servings: 20 Meatballs

Ingredients:

- 1 lb. lamb shoulder, ground
- Three garlic cloves, finely diced
- 3 tbsp. shallot, diced
- 1 tbsp. salt
- One egg
- 1/2 tbsp. pepper

- 1/2 tbsp. cumin

- 1/2 tbsp. smoked paprika

- 1/4 tbsp. red pepper flakes

- 1/4 tbsp. cinnamon

- 1/4 cup panko breadcrumbs

Directions:

1. Set your Pit Boss to 2500F.

2. Combine all the fixings in a small bowl, then mix thoroughly using your hands.

3. Form golf ball-sized meatballs and place them on a baking sheet.

4. Place the baking sheet in the smoker and smoke until the internal temperature reaches 1600F.

5. Remove the meatballs from the smoker and serve when hot.

Nutrition:

Calories 93

Total fat 5.9g

Total carbs 4.8g

Protein 5g

Sugars 0.3g

Fiber 0.3g

Sodium 174.1mg

Potassium 82.8mg

13. Pit Boss Crown Rack of Lamb
Preparation Time: 30 Minutes

Cooking Time: 30 Minutes

Servings: 6

Ingredients:

- Two racks of lamb. Frenched
- 1 tbsp garlic, crushed
- 1 tbsp rosemary
- 1/2 cup olive oil
- Kitchen twine

Directions:

1. Preheat your Pit Boss to 4500F.

2. Rinse the lab with clean cold water, then pat it dry with a paper towel.

3. Lay the lamb even on a chopping board and score a ¼ inch down between the bones. Repeat the process between the bones on each lamb rack. Set aside.

4. In a small mixing bowl, combine garlic, rosemary, and oil. Brush the lamb rack generously with the mixture.

5. Bend the lamb rack into a semicircle, then place the racks together such that the bones will be up and will form a crown shape.

6. Wrap around four times, starting from the base moving upward. Tie tightly to keep the racks together.

7. Place the lambs on a baking sheet and set in the Pit Boss. Cook on high heat for 10 minutes. Reduce the temperature to 3000F and cook for 20 more minutes or until the internal temperature reaches 1300F.

8. Remove the lamb rack from the Pit Boss and let rest while wrapped in a foil for 15 minutes.

9. Serve when hot.

Nutrition:

Calories 390

Total fat 35g

Total carbs 0g

Protein 17g

Sodium 65mg

14. Wood Pellet Chicken Breasts
Preparation Time: 10 minutes

Cooking Time: 15 minutes

Servings: 6

Ingredients:

- 3 chicken breasts
- 1 tbsp avocado oil
- 1/4 tbsp garlic powder
- 1/4 tbsp onion powder
- 3/4 tbsp salt
- 1/4 tbsp pepper

Directions:

1. Preheat your pellet to 375°F.
2. Half the chicken breasts lengthwise then coat with avocado oil.
3. With the spices, drizzle it on all sides to season
4. Drizzle spices to season the chicken
5. Put the chicken on top of the grill and begin to cook until its internal temperature approaches 165 degrees Fahrenheit
6. Put the chicken on top of the grill and begin to cook until it rises to a temperature of 165 degrees Fahrenheit
7. Serve and enjoy.

Nutrition:

Calories: 120 Cal

Fat: 4 g

Carbohydrates: 0 g

Protein: 19 g

Fiber: 0 g

15. Wood Pellet Smoked Spatchcock Turkey

Preparation Time: 30 minutes

Cooking Time: 1 hour and 45 minutes

Servings: 6

Ingredients:

- 1 whole turkey
- 1/2 cup oil
- 1/4 cup chicken rub
- 1 tbsp onion powder
- 1 tbsp garlic powder
- 1 tbsp rubbed sage

Directions:

1. Preheat your wood pellet grill to high.

2. Meanwhile, place the turkey on a platter with the breast side down then cut on either side of the backbone to remove the spine.

3. Flip the turkey and season on both sides then place it on the preheated grill or on a pan if you want to catch the drippings.

4.   Grill on high for 30 minutes, reduce the temperature to 325°F, and grill for 45 more minutes or until the internal temperature reaches 165°F

5.   Remove from the grill and let rest for 20 minutes before slicing and serving. Enjoy.

Nutrition:

Calories: 156 Cal

Fat: 16 g

Carbohydrates: 1 g

Protein: 2 g

Fiber: 0 g

16. Wood Pellet Smoked Cornish Hens
Preparation Time: 10 minutes

Cooking Time: 1 hour

Servings: 6

Ingredients:

- 6 Cornish hens
- 3 tbsp avocado oil
- 6 tbsp rub of choice

Directions:

1.   Fire up the wood pellet and preheat it to 275°F.

2.   Rub the hens with oil then coat generously with rub. Place the hens on the grill with the chest breast side down.

3.   Smoke for 30 minutes. Flip the hens and increase the grill temperature to 400°F. Cook until the internal temperature reaches 165°F.

4.   Remove from the grill and let rest for 10 minutes before serving. Enjoy.

Nutrition:

Calories: 696 Cal

Fat: 50 g

Carbohydrates: 1 g

Protein: 57 g

Fiber: 0 g

17. Smoked and Fried Chicken Wings
Preparation Time: 10 minutes

Cooking Time: 2 hours

Servings: 6

Ingredients:

- 3 pounds chicken wings
- 1 tbsp Goya adobo all-purpose seasoning
- Sauce of your choice

Directions:

1.   Fire up your wood pellet grill and set it to smoke.

2.   Meanwhile, coat the chicken wings with adobo all-purpose seasoning. Place the chicken on the grill and smoke for 2 hours.

3.   Remove the wings from the grill.

4. Preheat oil to 375°F in a frying pan. Drop the wings in batches and let fry for 5 minutes or until the skin is crispy.

5. Drain the oil and proceed with drizzling preferred sauce

6. Drain oil and drizzle preferred sauce

7. Enjoy.

Nutrition:

Calories: 755 Cal

Fat: 55 g

Carbohydrates: 24 g

Protein: 39 g

Fiber: 1 g

18. Wood Pellet Grilled Buffalo Chicken Leg

Preparation Time: 5 minutes

Cooking Time: 25 minutes

Servings: 6

Ingredients:

- 12 chicken legs
- 1/2 tbsp salt
- 1 tbsp buffalo seasoning
- 1 cup buffalo sauce

Directions:

1. Preheat your wood pellet grill to 325°F.

2.   Toss the legs in salt and buffalo seasoning then place them on the preheated grill.

3.   Grill for 40 minutes ensuring you turn them twice through the cooking.

4.   Brush the legs with buffalo sauce and cook for an additional 10 minutes or until the internal temperature reaches 165°F.

5.   Remove the legs from the grill, brush with more sauce, and serve when hot.

Nutrition:

Calories: 956 Cal

Fat: 47 g

Carbohydrates: 1 g

Protein: 124 g

Fiber: 0 g

19. Smoked Turkey Patties

Preparation Time: 20 minutes

Cooking Time: 40 minutes

Servings: 6

Ingredients:

- 2 lbs. turkey minced meat
- 1/2 cup of parsley finely chopped
- 2/3 cup of onion finely chopped
- 1 red bell pepper finely chopped
- 1 large egg at room temperature
- Salt and pepper to taste
- 1/2 tsp dry oregano
- 1/2 tsp dry thyme

Directions:

1. In a bowl, combine well all ingredients.
2. Make from the mixture patties.
3. Start Pit Boss grill on (recommended apple or oak Pit Boss) lid open, until the fire is established (4-5 minutes). Increase the temperature to 350F and allow to pre-heat, lid closed, for 10 - 15 minutes.
4. Place patties on the grill racks and cook with lid covered for 30 to 40 minutes.

5. Your turkey patties are ready when you reach a temperature of 130F

6. Serve hot.

Nutrition:

Calories: 251

Carbohydrates: 3.4g

Fat: 12.5

Fiber: 0.9g

Protein: 31.2g

20. Apple Smoked Turkey
Preparation Time: 30 Minutes

Cooking Time: 3 Hours

Servings: 5

Ingredients:

- 4 Cups Applewood chips

- 1 Fresh or frozen turkey of about 12 pounds

- 3 Tablespoons of extra-virgin olive oil

- 1 tablespoon of chopped fresh sage

- 2 and ½ teaspoons of kosher salt

- 2 Teaspoons of freshly ground black pepper

- 1 and ½ teaspoons of paprika

- 1 Teaspoon of chopped fresh thyme

- 1 Teaspoon of chopped fresh oregano

- 1 Teaspoon of garlic powder

- 1 Cup of water

- ½ Cup of chopped onion

- ½ Cup of chopped carrot

- ½ Cup of chopped celery

Directions:

1. Soak the wood chips into the water for about 1 hour; then drain very well.

2. Remove the neck and the giblets from the turkey; then reserve and discard the liver. Pat the turkey dry; then trim any excess of fat and start at the neck's cavity

3. Loosen the skin from the breast and the drumstick by inserting your fingers and gently push it between the meat and skin and lift the wingtips, then over back and tuck under the turkey

4. Combine the oil and the next 7 ingredients in a medium bowl and rub the oil under the skin; then rub it over the breasts and the drumsticks

5. Tie the legs with the kitchen string.

6. Pour 1 cup of water, the onion, the carrot, and the celery into the bottom of an aluminum foil roasting pan

7. Place the roasting rack into a pan; then arrange the turkey with the breast side up over a roasting rack; then let stand at the room temperature for about 1 hour

8. Remove the grill rack; then preheat the charcoal smoker grill to medium-high heat.

9. After preheating the smoker to a temperature of about 225°F

10. Place 2 cups of wood chips on the heating element on the right side.

11. Replace the grill rack; then place the roasting pan with the turkey over the grill rack over the left burner.

12. Cover and smoke for about 3 hours and turn the chicken halfway through the cooking time; then add the remaining 2 cups of wood chips halfway through the cooking time.

13. Place the turkey over a cutting board; then let stand for about 30 minutes

14. Discard the turkey skin; then serve and enjoy your dish!

Nutrition:

Calories: 530,

Fat: 22g,

Carbohydrates: 14g,

Protein: 41g,

Dietary Fiber 2g

21. Special Occasion's Dinner Cornish Hen

Preparation Time: 15 minutes

Cooking Time: 1 hour

Servings: 4

Ingredients:

- 4 Cornish game hens
- 4 fresh rosemary sprigs
- 4 tbsp. butter, melted

- 4 tsp. chicken rub

Directions:

1. Set the temperature of Grill to 375 degrees F and preheat with closed lid for 15 mins.

2. With paper towels, pat dry the hens.

3. Tuck the wings behind the backs and with kitchen strings, tie the legs together.

4. Coat the outside of each hen with melted butter and sprinkle with rub evenly.

5. Stuff each hen with a rosemary sprig.

6. Place the hens onto the grill and cook for about 50-60 mins.

7. Remove the hens from grill and place onto a platter for about 10 mins.

8. Cut each hen into desired-sized pieces and serve.

Nutrition:

Calories per serving: 430

Carbohydrates: 2.1g

Protein: 25.4g

Fat: 33g

Sugar: 0g

Sodium: 331mg

Fiber: 0.7g

22. Thanksgiving Dinner Turkey

Preparation Time: 15 minutes

Cooking Time: 4 hours

Servings: 16

Ingredients:

- ½ lb. butter, softened
- 2 tbsp. fresh thyme, chopped
- 2 tbsp. fresh rosemary, chopped
- 6 garlic cloves, crushed
- 1 (20-lb.) whole turkey, neck and giblets removed
- Salt and ground black pepper

Directions:

1. Set the temperature of Grill to 300 degrees F and preheat with closed lid for 15 mins, using charcoal.

2. In a bowl, place butter, fresh herbs, garlic, salt and black pepper and mix well.

3. Separate the turkey skin from breast to create a pocket.

4. Stuff the breast pocket with ¼-inch thick layer of butter mixture.

5. Season turkey with salt and black pepper.

6. Arrange the turkey onto the grill and cook for 3-4 hours.

7. Remove the turkey from grill and place onto a cutting board for about 15-20 mins before carving.

8. Cut the turkey into desired-sized pieces and serve.

Nutrition:

Calories per serving: 965

Carbohydrates: 0.6;

Protein: 106.5g

Fat: 52g

Sugar: 0g

Sodium: 1916mg

Fiber: 0.2g

23. Roasted Turkey with Herb

Preparation Time: 15 Minutes

Cooking Time: 3 Hours 30 Minutes

Servings: 12

Ingredients:

- 14 pounds turkey, cleaned
- 2 tablespoons chopped mixed herbs
- Pork and poultry rub as needed
- ¼ teaspoon ground black pepper
- 3 tablespoons butter, unsalted, melted
- 8 tablespoons butter, unsalted, softened
- 2 cups chicken broth

Directions:

1. Clean the turkey by removing the giblets, wash it inside out, pat dry with paper towels, then place it on a roasting pan and tuck the turkey wings by tiring with butcher's string.

2. Switch on the grill, fill the grill hopper with hickory flavored Pit Bosss, power the grill on by using the

control panel, select 'smoke' on the temperature dial, or set the temperature to 325 degrees F and let it preheat for a minimum of 15 minutes.

3. Meanwhile, prepared herb butter and for this, take a small bowl, place the softened butter in it, add black pepper and mixed herbs and beat until fluffy.

4. Place some of the prepared herb butter underneath the skin of turkey by using a handle of a wooden spoon, and massage the skin to distribute butter evenly.

5. Then rub the exterior of the turkey with melted butter, season with pork and poultry rub, and pour the broth in the roasting pan.

6. When the grill has preheated, open the lid, place roasting pan containing turkey on the grill grate, shut the grill and smoke for 3 hours and 30 minutes until the internal temperature reaches 165 degrees F and the top has turned golden brown.

7. When done, transfer turkey to a cutting board, let it rest for 30 minutes, then carve it into slices and serve.

Nutrition: Calories: 154.6 Fat: 3.1 g Carbs: 8.4 g Protein: 28.8 g

Fish and seafood recipes

24. Blackened Salmon
Preparation Time: 10 Minutes

Cooking Time: 20 Minutes

Servings: 4

Ingredients:

- 2 lb. salmon, fillet, scaled and deboned
- Two tablespoons olive oil
- Four tablespoons sweet dry rub
- One tablespoon cayenne pepper
- Two cloves garlic, minced

Directions:

1. Turn on your wood pellet grill.
2. Set it to 350 degrees F.
3. Brush the salmon with the olive oil.
4. Sprinkle it with the dry rub, cayenne pepper, and garlic.
5. Grill for 5 minutes per side.

Nutrition:

Calories 119

Total fat 10g

Saturated fat 2g

Sodium 720mg

25. Grilled Cajun Shrimp
Preparation Time: 5 Minutes

Cooking Time: 25 Minutes

Servings: 8

Ingredients:

Dip

- 1/2 cup mayonnaise
- One teaspoon lemon juice
- 1 cup sour cream
- One clove garlic, grated
- One tablespoon Cajun seasoning
- One tablespoon hickory bacon rub
- One tablespoon hot sauce
- Chopped scallions

Shrimp

- 1/2 lb. shrimp, peeled and deveined
- Two tablespoons olive oil
- 1/2 tablespoon hickory bacon seasoning
- One tablespoon Cajun seasoning

Directions:

1. Turn on your wood pellet grill.
2. Set it to 350 degrees F.
3. Mix the dip ingredients in a bowl.
4. Transfer to a small pan.
5. Cover with foil.
6. Place on top of the grill.

7. Cook for 10 minutes.

8. Coat the shrimp with the olive oil and sprinkle with the seasonings.

9. Grill for 5 minutes per side.

10. Pour the dip on top or serve with the shrimp.

Nutrition:

Calories 87

Total carbs 2g

Net carbs 2g

Protein 16g

Sodium 1241mg

26. Salmon Cakes

Preparation Time: 5 Minutes

Cooking Time: 25 Minutes

Servings: 4

Ingredients:

- 1 cup cooked salmon, flaked
- 1/2 red bell pepper, chopped
- Two eggs, beaten
- 1/4 cup mayonnaise
- 1/2 tablespoon dry sweet rub
- 1 1/2 cups breadcrumbs
- One tablespoon mustard
- Olive oil

Directions:

1. Combine all the fixings except the olive oil in a bowl.

2. Form patties from this mixture.

3. Let sit for 15 minutes.

4. Turn on your wood pellet grill.

5. Set it to 350 degrees F.

6. Add a baking pan to the grill.

7. Drizzle a little olive oil on top of the pan.

8. Add the salmon cakes to the pan.

9. Grill each side for 3 to 4 minutes.

Nutrition:

Calories 119

Total fat 10g

Saturated fat 2g

Sodium 720mg

27. Pineapple Maple Glaze Fish
Preparation Time: 10 minutes

Cooking Time: 15 Minutes

Servings: 6 Servings

Ingredients:

- 3 pounds of fresh salmon
- 1/4 cup maple syrup
- 1/2 cup pineapple juice
- Brine Ingredients

- 3 cups of water
- Sea salt, to taste
- 2 cups of pineapple juice
- ½ cup of brown sugar
- 5 tablespoons of Worcestershire sauce
- 1 tablespoon of garlic salt

Directions:

1. Combine all the brine ingredients in a large cooking pan.
2. Place the fish into the brine and let it sit for 2 hours for marinating.
3. After 2 hours, take out the fish and pat dry with a paper towel and set aside.
4. Preheat the smoker grill to 250 degrees Fahrenheit, until the smoke started to appear.
5. Put salmon on the grill and cook for 15 minutes.
6. Meanwhile, mix pineapple and maple syrup in a bowl and baste fish every 5 minutes.
7. Once the salmon is done, serve and enjoy.

Nutrition:

Calories 123

Total Fat 4.9g6 %

Saturated Fat 1.5g8 %

Cholesterol 60mg20 %

Sodium 29mg1 %

Total Carbohydrate 0g0 %

Dietary Fiber 0g0 %

Sugar 0g

28. Smoked Catfish Recipe
Preparation Time: 10 minutes

Cooking Time: 5 Minutes

Servings: 3 Servings

Ingredients:

Ingredients for The Rub

- 2 tablespoons paprika
- 1/4 teaspoon salt
- 1 tablespoon garlic powder
- 1 tablespoon onion powder
- 1/2 tablespoon dried thyme
- 1/2 tablespoon cayenne

Other ingredients

- 2 pounds fresh catfish fillets
- 4 tablespoons butter, soften

Directions:

1. Take a mixing bowl, and combine all the rub ingredients in it, including the paprika, salt, garlic powder, onion powder, and thyme and cayenne paper.
2. Rub the fillet with the butter, and then sprinkle a generous amount of rub on top
3. Coat fish well with the rub.
4. Preheat the smoker grill at 200 degrees Fahrenheit for 15 minutes.
5. Cook fish on the grill for 10 minutes, 5minutes per side.
6. Once done, serve and enjoy.

Nutrition:

Calories 146 - Total Fat 4.2g - Saturated Fat 2.5g - Cholesterol 61mg

Sodium 28mg

Vegetarian recipes

29. Grilled Corn with Honey Butter
Preparation Time: 15 minutes

Cooking Time: 10 minutes

Servings: 6

Ingredients:

- 6 pieces corn, husked

- 2 tablespoons olive oil

- Salt and pepper to taste

- ½ cup butter, room temperature

- ½ cup honey

Directions:

1. Fire the Pit Boss Grill to 3500F. Use desired wood pellets when cooking. Keep lid unopened to preheat until 15 minutes

2. Coat corn with oil and add salt and pepper

3. Place the corn on the grill grate and cook for 10 minutes. Make sure to flip the corn halfway through the cooking time for even cooking.

4. Meanwhile, mix the butter and honey on a small bowl. Set aside.

5. Remove corn from grill and coat with honey butter sauce

Nutrition:

Calories: 387 Cal

Fat: 21.6 g

Carbohydrates: 51.2 g

Protein: 5 g

Fiber: 0 g

30. Smoked Mushrooms
Preparation Time: 20 minutes

Cooking Time: 2 hours

Servings: 6

Ingredients:

- 6-12 large Portobello mushrooms
- Sea salt
- black pepper
- Extra virgin olive oil
- Herbs de Provence

Directions:

1. Preheat the smoker to 200°F while adding water and wood chips to the smoker bowl and tray, respectively.

2. Wash and dry mushrooms

3. Rub the mushrooms with olive oil, salt and pepper seasoning with herbs in a bowl.

4. Place the mushrooms with the cap side down on the smoker rack. Smoke the mushrooms for 2 hours while adding water and wood chips to the smoker after every 60 minutes.

5. Remove the mushrooms and serve

Nutrition:

Calories: 106 Cal

Fat: 6 g

Carbohydrates: 5 g

Protein: 8 g

Fiber: 0.9 g

31. Smoked Cherry Tomatoes
Preparation Time: 20 minutes

Cooking Time: 1 ½ hours

Servings: 8-10

Ingredients:

- 2 pints of tomatoes

Directions:

1. Preheat the electric smoker to 225°F while adding wood chips and water to the smoker.

2. Clean the tomatoes with clean water and dry them off properly.

3. Place the tomatoes on the pan and place the pan in the smoker.

4. Smoke for 90 minutes while adding water and wood chips to the smoker.

Nutrition:

Calories: 16 Cal

Fat: 0 g

Carbohydrates: 3 g

Protein: 1 g

Fiber: 1 g

32. Smoked and Smashed New Potatoes
Preparation Time: 5 minutes

Cooking Time: 8 hours

Servings: 4

Ingredients:

- 1-1/2 pounds small new red potatoes or fingerlings

- Extra virgin olive oil

- Sea salt and black pepper

- 2 tbsp softened butter

Directions:

1. Let the potatoes dry. Once dried, put in a pan and coat with salt, pepper, and extra virgin olive oil.

2. Place the potatoes on the topmost rack of the smoker.

3. Smoke for 60 minutes.

4. Once done, take them out and smash each one

5. Mix with butter and season

Nutrition:

Calories: 258 Cal

Fat: 2.0 g

Carbohydrates: 15.5 g

Protein: 4.1 g

Fiber: 1.5 g

33. Smoked Brussels Sprouts
Preparation Time: 15 minutes

Cooking Time: 45 minutes

Servings: 6

Ingredients:

- 1-1/2 pounds Brussels sprouts
- 2 cloves of garlic minced
- 2 tbsp extra virgin olive oil
- Sea salt and cracked black pepper

Directions:

1. Rinse sprouts
2. Remove the outer leaves and brown bottoms off the sprouts.
3. Place sprouts in a large bowl then coat with olive oil.
4. Add a coat of garlic, salt, and pepper and transfer them to the pan.
5. Add to the top rack of the smoker with water and woodchips.
6. Smoke for 45 minutes or until reaches 250°F temperature.
7. Serve

Nutrition:

Calories: 84 Cal

Fat: 4.9 g

Carbohydrates: 7.2 g

Protein: 2.6 g

Fiber: 2.9 g

Vegan recipes

34. Wood Pellet Smoked Acorn Squash

Preparation Time: 10 minutes

Cooking Time: 2 hours

Servings: 6

Ingredients:

- 3 tbsp. olive oil
- 3 acorn squash, halved and seeded
- 1/4 cup unsalted butter
- 1/4 cup brown Sugar:
- 1 tbsp. cinnamon, ground
- 1 tbsp. chili powder
- 1 tbsp. nutmeg, ground

Directions:

1. Brush olive oil on the acorn squash cut sides then covers the halves with foil. Poke holes on the foil to allow steam and smoke through.
2. Fire up the wood pellet to 225°F and smoke the squash for 1 ½-2 hours.
3. Remove the squash from the smoker and allow it to sit.
4. Meanwhile, melt butter, Sugar: and spices in a saucepan. Stir well to combine.
5. Remove the foil from the squash and spoon the butter mixture in each squash half. Enjoy.

Nutrition:

Calories: 149

Total Fat: 10g

Saturated Fat: 5g

Total Carbs: 14g

Net Carbs: 12g

Protein: 2g

Sugar: 0g

Fiber: 2g

Sodium: 19mg

Potassium: 0mg

Snack and appetizer recipes

35. Corn Salsa

Preparation Time: 10 Minutes

Cooking Time: 15 Minutes

Servings: 4

Ingredients:

- 4 Ears Corn, large with the husk on
- 4 Tomatoes (Roma) diced and seeded
- 1 tsp. of Onion powder
- 1 tsp. of Garlic powder
- 1 Onion, diced
- ½ cup chopped Cilantro
- Black pepper and salt to taste
- 1 lime, the juice
- 1 grille jalapeno, diced

Directions:

1. Preheat the grill to 450F.

2. Place the ears corn on the grate and cook until charred. Remove husk. Cut into kernels.

3. Combine all ingredients, plus the corn and mix well. Refrigerate before serving.

4. Enjoy!

Nutrition: Calories: 120 Protein: 2f Carbs: 4g Fat: 1g

36. Nut Mix on the Grill

Preparation Time: 15 Minutes

Cooking Time: 20 Minutes

Servings: 8

Ingredients:

- 3 cups Mixed Nuts, salted
- 1 tsp. Thyme, dried
- 1 ½ tbsp. brown sugar, packed
- 1 tbsp. Olive oil
- ¼ tsp. of Mustard powder
- ¼ tsp. Cayenne pepper

Directions:

1. Preheat the grill to 250F with closed lid.

2. In a bowl combine the ingredients and place the nuts on a baking tray lined with parchment paper. Place the try on the grill. Cook 20 minutes.

3. Serve and enjoy!

Nutrition: Calories: 65 Protein: 23g Carbs 4g: Fat: 52g

37. Grilled Corn

Preparation Time: 15 minutes

Cooking Time: 25 minutes

Servings: 6

Ingredients:

- Six fresh ears of corn
- Salt
- Black pepper
- Olive oil
- Vegetable seasoning
- Butter for serving

Directions:

1. Preheat the grill to high with a closed lid.
2. Peel the husks. Remove the corn's silk. Rub with black pepper, salt, vegetable seasoning, and oil.

3.   Close the husks and grill for 25 minutes. Turn them occasionally.
4.   Serve topped with butter and enjoy.

Nutrition: Calories: 70 Protein: 3g Carbs: 18g Fat: 2g

38. Thyme - Rosemary Mash Potatoes

Preparation Time: 20 minutes

Cooking Time: 1 hour

Servings: 6

Ingredients:

- 4 ½ lbs. Potatoes, russet
- Salt
- 1 pint of Heavy cream
- 3 Thyme sprigs + 2 tablespoons for garnish
- 2 Rosemary sprigs
- 6 - 7 Sage leaves
- 6 - 7 Black peppercorns
- Black pepper to taste
- Two stick Butter softened
- 2 Garlic cloves, chopped

Directions:

1.   Preheat the grill to 350F with a closed lid.
2.   Peel the russet potatoes.
3.   Cut into small pieces and place them in a baking dish. Fill it with water (1 ½ cups). Place on the grill and cook with a closed lid for about 1 hour.
4.   In the meantime, in a saucepan, combine the garlic, peppercorns, herbs, and cream. Place on the grate and cook covered for about 15 minutes. Once done, strain to remove the garlic and herbs. Keep warm.
5.   Take out the water of the potatoes and place them in a stockpot. Rice them with a fork and pour 2/3 of the mixture. Add one stick of softened butter and salt.

6.   Serve right away.

Nutrition: Calories: 180 Protein: 4g Carbs: 28g Fat: 10g

39. Cinnamon Almond Shortbread

Preparation Time: 20 minutes

Cooking Time: 20 minutes

Servings: 5

Ingredients:

- 2tsp cinnamon
- ½ cup unsalted butter (softened)
- 1large egg (beaten)
- ½ tsp salt or to taste
- 2cups almond flour
- ¼ cup sugar
- 1tsp ginger (optional)

Directions:

1. Preheat the grill to 300°F with the lid closed for 5 minutes.

2. Grease a cookie sheet with oil.

3. In a large bowl, combine the cinnamon, almond flour, sugar, ginger, and salt. Mix thoroughly to combine.

4. In another mixing bowl, whisk the egg and softened butter together.

5. Pour the egg mixture into the flour mixture and mix until the mixture forms a smooth batter.

6. Use a tablespoon to measure out equal amounts of the mixture and roll into balls.

7. Arrange the balls into the cookie sheet in a single layer.

8. Now, use the flat bottom of a clean glass cup to press each ball into a flat round cookie. Grease the bottom of the cup before using it to press the balls.

9. Place the cookie sheet on the grill and bake until browned. This will take about 20 to 25 minutes.

10. Remove the cookie sheet from the grill and let the shortbreads cool for a few minutes.

11. Serve and enjoy.

Nutrition: Calories: 152 Total Fat: 12.7 g Saturated Fat: 4.2 g Cholesterol: 27 mg Sodium: 124 mg Total Carbohydrate: 6.5 g Dietary Fiber: 1.7 g Total Sugars: 3.2 g Protein: 3.5 g

40. Simple Roasted Butternut Squash
Preparation Time: 5 minutes

Cooking Time: 25 minutes

Servings: 8

Ingredients:

- 1(2 pounds) butternut squash
- 2garlic cloves (minced)
- 2tablespoon extra olive virgin oil
- 1tsp paprika
- 1tsp oregano
- 1tsp thyme
- Salt and pepper to taste

Directions:

1. Start your grill on smoke mode and leave the grill open for 5 minutes, until fire Preheat the grill to 400°F.

2. Peel the butternut squash.

3. Cut the butternut squash into two (cut lengthwise).

4. Use a spoon to scoop out the seeds.

5. Cut the butternut squash into 1-inch chunks and wash the chunks with water.

6. In a big bowl, combine the butternut squash chunks and other ingredients.

7. Stir until the chunks are coated with the ingredients.

8. Spread the coated chunks on the sheet pan.

9. Place the sheet pan on the grill and bake for 25 minutes.

10. Remove the baked butternut squash from heat and let it sit to cool.

11. Serve.

Nutrition: Calories: 8 Total Fat: 3.7 g Saturated Fat: 0.5 g Cholesterol: 0 mg Sodium: 331 mg Total Carbohydrate 13.8 g Dietary Fiber 2.6 g Total Sugars: 2.5 g Protein: 1.2 g

Baking recipes

41. Fruits on Bread
Preparation Time: 30 minutes

Cooking Time: 1 hour and 30 minutes

Servings: 8

Ingredients:

- 1/2 cup milk

- 1 teaspoon sugar

- 1/4 cup warm water

- 2 1/2 teaspoon active yeast, instant

- 2 1/2 cups all-purpose flour

- 2 tablespoon melted butter

- 1 egg

- 1/2 teaspoon vanilla

- 1/2 teaspoon salt

- Vegetable oil

- 1 tablespoon ground cinnamon

- Chocolate spread

- Fruits, sliced

Directions:

1. Add the milk, sugar, water and yeast in a bowl. Let sit for 10 minutes.

2. In another bowl, add the flour.

3. Create a well in the center.

4. Add the sugar mixture, butter, egg, vanilla and salt.

5. Mix and knead.

6. Place in a bowl.

7. Cover with clean towel.

8. Let rise for 1 hour.

9. Start your wood pellet grill.

10. Set it to 450 degrees F.

11. Grease a cast iron skillet with the oil.

12. Create balls from the mixture.

13. Press and sprinkle with the cinnamon.

14. Fry for 1 minute per side.

15. Spread with chocolate and top with sliced fruits.

Nutrition:

Calories: 110 Cal

Fat: 2 g

Carbohydrates: 21 g

Protein: 5 g

Fiber: 2 g

42. Grilled Steak with American Cheese Sandwich

Preparation Time: 10 minutes

Cooking Time: 55 minutes

Servings: 4

Ingredients

1 pound of beef steak.

1/2 teaspoon of salt to taste.

1/2 teaspoon of pepper to taste.

1 tablespoon of Worcestershire sauce.

2 tablespoons of butter.

1 chopped onion.

1/2 chopped green bell pepper.

Salt and pepper to taste.

8 slices of American Cheese.

8 slices of white bread.

4 tablespoons of butter.

Directions:

Turn your Pit Boss Smoker and Grill to smoke and fire up for about four to five minutes. Set the temperature of the grill to 450 degrees F and let it preheat for about ten to fifteen minutes with its lid closed.

Next, place a non-stick skillet on the griddle and preheat for about fifteen minutes until it becomes hot. Once hot, add in the butter and let melt. Once the butter melts, add in the onions and green bell pepper then cook for about five minutes until they become brown in color, set aside.

Next, still using the same pan on the griddle, add in the steak, Worcestershire sauce, salt, and pepper to taste then cook for about five to six minutes until it is cooked through. Add in the cooked bell pepper mixture; stir to combine then heat for another three minutes, set aside.

Use a sharp knife to slice the bread in half, butter each side then grill for about three to four minutes with its sides down. To assemble, add slices of cheese on each bread slice, top with the steak mixture then your favorite toppings, close the sandwich with another bread slice then serve.

Nutrition:

Calories 589 cal

Carbohydrates 28g

Protein 24g

Fat 41g

Fiber 2g

43. Ground Turkey Burgers

Preparation Time: 15 minutes

Cooking Time: 50 minutes

Servings: 6

Ingredients

> beaten egg

2/3 cup of bread crumbs.

1/2 cup of chopped celery

1/4 cup of chopped onion

1 tablespoon of minced parsley

1 teaspoon of Worcestershire sauce

1 teaspoon of dried oregano

1/2 teaspoon of salt to taste

1/4 teaspoon of pepper

1-1/4 pounds of lean ground turkey

6 hamburger buns

Optional topping

1 sliced tomato

1 sliced onion

Lettuce leaves

Directions:

Using a small mixing bowl, add in all the ingredients on the list aside from the turkey and buns then mix properly to combine.

73

Add in the ground turkey then mix everything to combine. Feel free to use clean hands for this. Make about six patties of the mixture then set aside.

Preheat your Pit Boss Smoker and Grill to 375 degrees F, place the turkey patties on the grill and grill for about forty-five minutes until its internal temperature reads 165 degrees F. to assemble, use a knife to split the bun into two, top with the prepared burger and your favorite topping then close with another half of the buns, serve.

Nutrition:

Calories 293 cal

Fat 11g

Carbohydrate 27g

Fiber 4g

Protein 22g

44. Fancy Taco Seasoning
Preparation Time: 10 minutes

Cooking Time: Nil

Serving: 4

Ingredients

- 1 tablespoon of Chili powder
- ½ a teaspoon of Garlic powder
- ½ a teaspoon of Onion powder
- 1 and a ½ teaspoon of ground cumin
- 1 teaspoon of salt
- 1 teaspoon of pepper
- ¼ teaspoon of crushed red pepper flakes
- ¼ teaspoon of dried oregano
- ½ a teaspoon of paprika

Directions:

1. Mix the ingredients mentioned above to prepare the Taco seasoning and use it as needed.

   Nutrition:

   Calories: 10

   Carbs: 7g

   Protein: 2g

45. Special BBQ Sauce
Preparation Time: 10 minutes

Cooking Time: Nil

Serving: 4

Ingredients

- ½ a cup of apple cider vinegar
- 2 tablespoons of water
- 2 tablespoon of coconut aminos

- ¼ teaspoon of mustard seeds
- ¼ teaspoon of onion powder
- ¼ teaspoon of garlic powder
- 1/8 teaspoon of cinnamon
- 1/8 teaspoon of black pepper

Directions:

1. Add all the listed ingredients to your saucepan
2. Bring it to a boil and stir well
3. Simmer for a few minutes
4. Remove the heat and allow it to cool
5. Use as needed!

Nutrition:

Calories: 10

Carbs: 7g

Protein: 2g

46. Classic Home-Made Worcestershire Sauce
Preparation Time: 10 minutes

Cooking Time: 15 minutes

Serving: 4

Ingredients

- ½ a cup of apple cider vinegar
- 2 tablespoons of water
- 2 tablespoon of coconut aminos
- ¼ teaspoon of mustard seeds
- ¼ teaspoon of onion powder
- ¼ teaspoon of garlic powder
- 1/8 teaspoon of cinnamon
- 1/8 teaspoon of black pepper

Directions:

1. Add all the listed ingredients to your saucepan
2. Bring it to a boil and stir well

3. Simmer for a few minutes
4. Remove the heat and allow it to cool
5. Use as needed!

Nutrition:

Calories: 10

Carbs: 7g

Protein: 2g

47. Original Ketchup
Preparation Time: 10 minutes

Cooking Time: 20 minutes

Serving: 4

Ingredients

- ½ a cup of chopped pitted dates
- 1 can of 6-ounce tomato paste
- 1 can of 14-ounce diced tomatoes
- 2 tablespoon of coconut vinegar
- ½ a cup of bone broth
- 1 teaspoon of garlic powder
- 1 teaspoon of onion powder
- 1 teaspoon of salt
- ½ a teaspoon of cayenne pepper

Directions:

1. Add the ingredients to a small-sized saucepan
2. Cook on medium-low for 20 minutes
3. Remove the heat
4. Take an immersion blender and blend the mixture until smooth
5. Remove the mixer and simmer on low for 10 minutes
6. Use as needed

Nutrition:

Calories: 10

Carbs: 7g

Protein: 2g

48. Lovely Mayonnaise
Preparation Time: 10 minutes

Cooking Time: Nil

Serving: 4

Ingredients

- 1 whole egg
- ½ a teaspoon of sea salt
- ½ a teaspoon of ground mustard
- 1 and a ¼ cup of extra light olive oil
- 1 tablespoon of lemon juice

Directions:

1. Place the egg, ground mustard, salt and ¼ cup of olive oil into a food processor
2. Whirl on low until mixed
3. While the processor is running, drizzle remaining olive oil and keep whirling for 3 minutes
4. Add lemon juice and pulse on low until thoroughly mixed
5. Chill for 30 minutes
6. Use as needed

Nutrition:

Calories: 10

Carbs: 7g

Protein: 2g

Dessert recipes

49. Ice Cream Bread

Preparation Time: 10 Minutes

Cooking Time: 1 Hour

Servings: 12-16

Ingredients:

- 1 ½ quart full-fat butter pecan ice cream, softened
- One t. salt
- Two c. semisweet chocolate chips
- One c. sugar
- One stick melted butter
- Butter, for greasing
- 4 c. self-rising flour

Directions:

1. Add wood pellets to your smoker and follow your cooker's startup program. Preheat your smoker, with your lid closed, until it reaches 350.

2. Set the cake on the grill, cover, and smoke for 50 minutes to an hour. A toothpick should come out clean.

3. Take the pan off of the grill. For 10 mins., cool the bread.

Nutrition:

Calories: 135

Carbs: 0g

Fat: 0g

Protein: 0g

50. Mediterranean Meatballs
Preparation Time: 15 Minutes

Cooking Time: 35 Minutes

Servings: 8

Ingredients:

- Pepper
- Salt
- One t. vinegar
- Two T. olive oil
- Two eggs
- One chopped onion
- One soaked slice of bread
- ½ t. cumin
- One T. chopped basil
- 1 ½ T. chopped parsley
- 2 ½ pounds ground beef

Directions:

1. Use your hands to combine everything until thoroughly combined. If needed, when forming meatballs, dip your hands into some water. Shape into 12 meatballs.

2. Add wood pellets to your smoker.

3. Preheat your smoker, with your lid closed, until it reaches 380.

4. Place the meatballs onto the grill and cook on all sides for eight minutes. Take off the grill and let sit for five minutes.

5. Serve with favorite condiments or a salad.

Nutrition:

Calories: 33

Carbs: 6g

Fat: 0g

Protein: 1g

51. Greek Meatballs
Preparation Time: 10 Minutes

Cooking Time: 40 Minutes

Servings: 6

Ingredients:

- Pepper
- Salt
- Two chopped green onions
- One T. almond flour
- Two eggs
- ½ pound ground pork
- 2 ½ pound ground beef

Directions:

1. Mix all the ingredients using your hands until everything is incorporated evenly. Form mixture into meatballs until all meat is used.

2. Add wood pellets to your smoker and follow your cooker's startup procedure. Preheat your smoker, with your lid closed, until it reaches 380.

3. Brush the meatballs with olive oil and place onto the grill—Cook for ten minutes on all sides.

Nutrition:

Calories: 161

Carbs: 10g

Fat: 6g

Protein: 17g

Conclusion

The Pit boss pellet grill has made grilling simpler and safer for humanity, and grilling, which is part of "dietetic" cooking, has been made easier by the Pit boss grill. Providing us with the delicious meal we have been missing and thereby enhancing our quality of life. This book contains a variety of recipes that you can cook at home using your new Pit boss Pellet grill. The tenderness and tasty BBQ in the recipes can provide a lot of satisfaction.

The Pit boss barbecues are electric, and they are regulated by a standard 3-position mechanism. A cylindrical unit, like a pellet stove, transports pellets from the storage to the fireplace. The Pit boss Grill smoker ensures that your meat and other recipes work out perfectly. This smoker creates a wonderful atmosphere for your food. To achieve such a genuine flavor, high-quality materials and precise smoking are needed. It is best if you can reach the highest degree of smoking accuracy possible so that your meat and other recipes work out perfectly. Furthermore, if you want to add more spice to your recipes, use the best wood pellet for cooking.

Many people ask me why I choose Pit boss pellet grills, and you would think, well, the answer is easy and straightforward, and yes! It is right in front of us. What is the explanation for this?

It cooks over a wood fire, resulting in exceptional flavor because nothing compares real wood, real smoking, and natural aroma. The cooking method has evolved significantly. Expert chefs are known for experimenting with different flavors and ingredients to produce a delectable and tasty dish.

Grilling is one of the most common cooking methods for achieving a perfect flavor in your dishes. Grilling is a better cooking method than others because it benefits the food, retains flavor, and preserves nutrients. A Pit boss grill smoker's wood pellet grill, on the other hand, helps you to grill your food easily and with less effort and smoke. The benefit of having a Pit boss grill smoker in your home is that it is flexible, helps you cook food faster, offers a temperature control scale, and is one of the most critical aspects of cooking.

It is a flexible grill. In fact, the Pit boss grill smoker can be used to grill, smoke, bake, roast, and stew everything you can think of. This Pit boss grill smoker is a powerful tool that offers excellent service.

As we can all attest, Pit boss has made using the pellet grill simple: its intuitive control panel has a power button and a knob that allows you to easily change the temperature.

Finally, we should add that we can always find new flavors in our dishes through grilling: you can smoke your dishes with Pit boss pellets, giving them a constantly new and different taste. The Pit boss Grill smoker is the answer to your taste buds' prayers. Do not waste any more time; get your own smoker and begin cooking your favorite recipes with this book.

THE 2021 WOOD PELLET MASTERY COOKBOOK

2 Books in 1: The New Complete Guide for Perfect Smoking and Grilling | 100+ Quick and Easy Recipes That Your Family Will Love

Introduction

Pit boss grills and smokers are outdoor charcoal grills and smokers that use flavored wood pellets as fuel. Since it does not need gas or electricity, it is an environmentally friendly cooking alternative. You can enjoy fresh outdoor cooking using your own ingredients with this setup. As a result, it is a better choice because you can monitor the amount of nicotine and preservatives in your meal.

By using high-quality products and producing a product with a large brewing power, the business has gained a good reputation. Smoking any form of food is simple with a Pit Boss grill. Small, medium, and high temperatures are among the choices for smoking temperature provided by the company. Various models for smoking with various wood pellets or smoking methods are available. These are perfect for beginners who need to warm up before beginning a meal, as well as seasoned chefs who want to try out new meat flavors.

This Pit Boss Pellet Grill Review will give you a thorough understanding of the grill's key features. You'll find that it has a sleek design and a stylish exterior that makes it both attractive and practical. It's also transportable. As previously mentioned, you can use electricity or wood pellets to power this grill, and its high-quality construction ensures its longevity.

You'll also be able to enjoy every feature because this smoker is made of professional-grade materials, ensuring long-term use. It can handle a wide range of foods, including delicate things such as fish and meat. This grill will appeal to any taste while keeping the food safe.

To ensure that you understand how to use the product properly, a Pit boss grill analysis should provide a detailed description of the controls and service. You'll be able to hear about its features and versatility. Many people have saved money thanks to the various settings that enable them to monitor cooking times and heat levels according to their preferences. This could be a good choice for you if you want your food cooked perfectly inside and out, as it comes with very high-quality design specifications. A display window and a temperature gauge are both useful features.

Since this is an open-air smoker, food may need enough room for smoking when cooked at lower temperatures. Because of the temperature regulation, you will achieve the desired results. Since you are not in direct contact with the flames, you will still be able to keep your food safe. It is safe to use and there is no chance of spilling or steaming food. Because of its flavor and moisture content, the smoke is one-of-a-kind.

Pit Boss's proprietary "velocity cooking" smoker technology produces delicious food without the use of wood chips or charcoal. As a result, no chimney or charcoal starter kits are needed when using this grill. The pellets are lit using a simple push-button controller that helps you retain your ideal cooking temperature for longer than conventional grills.

The Pit Boss Grill features a unique design for easy access to the temperature controls. This allows you to adjust the temperature with ease, and it also provides your guests with an excellent view. The steel construction ensures that it can withstand the heat of the fire while the stainless steel finishing ensures that it will look great for years to come.

Pit Boss Grills are made with multiple vents to provide cooking space even under a heavy load. They feature a non-stick finish for easy cleaning and a stainless steel drip pan to catch the grease that makes it through the grate. Our grills are ready for whatever you're going to throw at them! Order yours today!

52. BBQ Beef Short Ribs

Preparation Time: 15 minutes

Cooking Time: 10 hours

Servings: 8

Ingredients:

- 4 beef short rib racks, membrane removed, containing 4 bones

- 1/2 cup beef rub

- 1 cup apple juice

Directions:

1. Switch on the Pit Boss grill, fill the grill hopper with apple-flavored Pit Bosss, power the grill on by using the control panel, select 'smoke' on the temperature dial, or set the temperature to 225 degrees F and let it preheat for a minimum of 15 minutes.

2. Meanwhile, prepare the ribs, and for this, sprinkle beef rub on both sides until well coated.

3. When the grill has preheated, open the lid, place ribs on the grill grate bone-side down, shut the grill, and smoke for 10 hours until internal temperature reaches 205 degrees F, spritzing with apple juice every hour.

4. When done, transfer ribs to a cutting board, let rest for 10 minutes, then cut into slices and serve.

Nutrition:

Calories: 280 Cal

Fat: 15 g

Carbs: 17 g

Protein: 20 g

Fiber: 1 g

53. Thai Beef Salad

Preparation Time: 10 minutes

Cooking Time: 10 minutes

Servings: 4

Ingredients:

- 1 ½ pound skirt steak
- 1 ½ teaspoon salt
- 1 teaspoon ground white pepper
- 4 jalapeño peppers, minced
- ½ teaspoon minced garlic
- 4 tablespoons Thai fish sauce
- 4 tablespoons lime juice
- 1 tablespoon brown sugar
- 1 small red onion, peeled, thinly sliced
- 6 cherry tomatoes, halved
- 2 green onions, ¼-inch diced
- 1 cucumber, deseeded, thinly sliced
- 1 heart of romaine lettuce, chopped
- ½ cup chopped mint
- 2 tablespoons cilantro
- ½ teaspoon red pepper flakes
- 1 tablespoon lime juice

- 2 tablespoons fish sauce

Directions:

1. Switch on the Pit Boss grill, fill the grill hopper with cherry flavored Pit Bosss, power the grill on by using the control panel, select 'smoke' on the temperature dial, or set the temperature to 450 degrees F and let it preheat for a minimum of 15 minutes.

2. Take a large salad, place all the ingredients for the salad in it, drizzle with dressing and toss until well coated and mixed.

3. When done, transfer steak to a cutting board, let it rest for 10 minutes and then cut it into slices.

4. Add steak slices into the salad, toss until mixed, and then serve.

Nutrition:

Calories: 128 Cal

Fat: 6 g

Carbs: 6 g

Protein: 12 g

Fiber: 1 g

54. Pit Boss Smoked Beef Jerky
Preparation Time: 15 minutes

Cooking Time: 5 hours

Servings: 10

Ingredients:

- 3 lb sirloin steaks, sliced into 1/4 inch thickness

- 2 cups soy sauce

- 1/2 cup brown sugar

- 1 cup pineapple juice

- 2 Tablespoon sriracha

- 2 Tablespoon red pepper flake

- 2 Tablespoon hoisin

- 2 Tablespoon onion powder

- 2 Tablespoon rice wine vinegar

- 2 Tablespoon garlic, minced

Direction:

1. Mix all the ingredients in a zip lock bag. Seal the bag and mix until the beef is well coated. Ensure you get as much air as possible from the zip lock bag.

2. Put the bag in the fridge overnight to let marinate. Remove the bag from the fridge 1 hour prior to cooking.

3. Startup your wood pallet grill and set it to smoke setting. Layout the meat on the grill with half-inch space between them.

4. Let them cook for 5 hours while turning after every 2-1/2 hours.

5. Transfer from the grill and let cool for 30 minutes before serving.

Nutrition:

Calories 80,

Total fat 1g,

Protein 14g,

Sugar 5g,

Fiber 0g,

Sodium: 650mg

55. Grilled Butter Basted Porterhouse Steak

Preparation Time: 15 minutes

Cooking Time: 40 minutes

Servings: 4

Ingredients:

- 4 Tablespoon butter, melted
- 2 Tablespoon Worcestershire sauce
- 2 Tablespoon Dijon mustard
- Pit Boss Prime rib rub

Direction:

1. Set your Pit Boss grill to 225°F with the lid closed for 15 minutes.

2. In a mixing bowl, mix butter, sauce, dijon mustard until smooth. brush the mixture on the meat then season with the rub.

3. Arrange the meat on the grill grate and cook for 30 minutes.

4. Use tongs to transfer the meat to a patter then increase the heat to high.

5. Return the meat to the grill grate to grill until your desired doneness is achieved.

6. Baste with the butter mixture again if you desire and let rest for 3 minutes before serving. Enjoy.

Nutrition:

Calories 726,

Total fat 62g,

Protein 36g,

Sugar 1g,

Fiber 1g,

Sodium: 97mg,

56. Pit Boss Grill Prime Rib Roast

Preparation Time: 5 minutes

Cooking Time: 4 hours

Servings: 10

Ingredients:

- 7 lb bone prime rib roast
- Pit Boss prime rib rub

Direction:

1. Coat the roast generously with the rub then wrap in a plastic wrap. let sit in the fridge for 24 hours to marinate.

2. Set the temperatures to 500°F.to to preheat with the lid closed for 15 minutes.

3. Place the rib directly on the grill fat side up and cook for 30 minutes.

4. Reduce the temperature to 300°F and cook for 4 hours or until the internal temperature is 120°F- rare, 130°F-medium rare, 140°F-medium and 150°F-well done.

5. Remove from the grill and let rest for 30 minutes then serve and enjoy.

Nutrition:

Calories 290,

Total fat 23g,

Protein 19g,

Sugar 0g,

Fiber 0g,

Sodium: 54mg,

57. Pit Boss Grill Teriyaki Beef Jerky

Preparation Time: 15 minutes

Cooking Time: 5 hours

Servings: 10

Ingredients:

- 3 cups soy sauce

- 2 cups brown sugar

- 3 garlic cloves

- 2-inch ginger knob, peeled and chopped

- 1 Tablespoon sesame oil

- 4 lb beef, skirt steak

Direction:

1. Place all the ingredients except the meat in a food processor. Pulse until well mixed.

2. Trim any excess fat from the meat and slice into 1/4 inch slices. Add the steak with the marinade into a zip lock bag and let marinate for 12-24 hours in a fridge.

3. Set the Pit Boss grill to smoke and let preheat for 5 minutes.

4. Arrange the steaks on the grill leaving a space between each. Let smoke for 5 hours.

5. Remove the steak from grill and serve when warm.

Nutrition:

Calories 80,

Total fat 1g,

Protein 11g,

Sugar 6g,

Fiber 0g,

Sodium: 390mg

58. Smoked Avocado Pork Ribs
Preparation Time: 20 Minutes

Cooking Time: 3 Hours

Servings: 5

Ingredients:

- 2 lbs. of pork spare ribs
- 1 cup of avocado oil
- One teaspoon of garlic powder
- One teaspoon of onion powder
- One teaspoon of sweet pepper flakes
- Salt and pepper, to taste

Directions:

1. In a bowl, combine the avocado oil, garlic salt, garlic powder, onion powder, sweet pepper flakes, and salt and pepper.

2. Place pork chops in a shallow container and pour evenly avocado mixture.

3. Cover and refrigerate for at least 4 hours or overnight.

4. Start pellet grill on, lid open until the fire is established (4-5 minutes).

5. Increase the temperature to 225 and pre-heat for 10 - 15 minutes.

6. Arrange pork chops on the grill rack and smoke for 3 to 4 hours.

7. Transfer pork chops on serving plate, let them rest for 15 minutes, and serve.

Nutrition:

Calories: 677 call

Carbohydrates: 0.9g

Fat: 64g

Fiber: 0.14g

Protein: 28.2g

59. Smoked Honey - Garlic Pork Chops
Preparation Time: 15 Minutes

Cooking Time: 60 Minutes

Servings: 4

Ingredients:

- 1/4 cup of lemon juice freshly squeezed
- 1/4 cup honey (preferably a darker honey)
- Three cloves garlic, minced
- Two tablespoons of soy sauce (or tamari sauce)
- Salt and pepper to taste
- 24 ounces center-cut pork chops boneless

Directions:

1. Combine honey, lemon juice, soy sauce, garlic, and salt and pepper in a bowl.

2. Place pork in a container and pour marinade over pork.

3. Cover and marinate in a fridge overnight.

4. Remove pork from marinade and pat dry on kitchen paper towel. (Reserve marinade)

5. Start your pellet on Smoke with the lid open until the fire is established (4 - 5 minutes).

6. Increase temperature to 450 and preheat, lid closed, for 10 - 15 minutes.

7. Arrange the pork chops on the grill racks and smoke for about one hour (depending on the thickness)

8. In the meantime, heat the remaining marinade in a small saucepan over medium heat to simmer.

9. Transfer pork chops on a serving plate, pour with the marinade, and serve hot.

Nutrition:

Calories: 301.5 call

Carbohydrates: 17g

Fat: 6.5g

Fiber: 0.2g

Protein: 41g

60. Smoked Pork Burgers
Preparation Time: 15 Minutes

Cooking Time: 1 Hour and 45 Minutes

Servings: 4

Ingredients:

- 2 lb. ground pork

- 1/2 of onion finely chopped

- 2 Tablespoon fresh sage, chopped

- One teaspoon garlic powder

- One teaspoon cayenne pepper

- Salt and pepper to taste

Directions:

1. Start the pellet grill on SMOKE wait until the fire is established.

2. Set the temperature to 225 and warm-up, lid closed, for 10 to 15 minutes.

3. In a bowl, combine ground pork with all remaining ingredients.

4. Use your hands to mix thoroughly—form mixture into eight evenly burgers.

5. Place the hamburgers on the racks.

6. Smoke the burgers for 60 minutes until they reach an internal temperature of 150 to 160.

7. Serve hot.

Nutrition:

Calories: 588.7 call

Carbohydrates: 1g

Fat: 48.2g

Fiber: 0.5g

Protein: 38.4g

61. Smoked Pork Chops Marinated with Tarragon
Preparation Time: 20 Minutes

Cooking Time: 3 Hours

Servings: 4

Ingredients:

- 1/2 cup olive oil
- 4 Tablespoon of fresh tarragon chopped
- Two teaspoons fresh thyme, chopped
- Salt and grated black pepper
- Two teaspoon apple cider vinegar
- Four pork chops or fillets

Directions:

1. Whisk the olive oil, tarragon, thyme, salt, pepper, apple cider, and stir well.
2. Place the pork chops in a container and pour it with a tarragon mixture.
3. Refrigerate for 2 hours.
4. Start pellet grill on, lid open, until the discharge is established (4-5 minutes). Increase the temperature to 225 and allow to pre-heat, lid closed, for 10 - 15 minutes.
5. Remove chops from marinade and pat dry on kitchen towel.
6. Arrange pork chops on the grill rack and smoke for 2 to 3 hours.
7. Transfer chops on a serving platter and lets it rest 15 minutes before serving.

Nutrition:

Calories: 528.8 Cal

Carbohydrates: 0.6g

Fat: 35g

Fiber: 0.14g

Protein: 51g

62. Grilled Lamb Burgers
Preparation Time: 10 minutes

Cooking Time: 15 minutes

Servings: 5

Ingredients:

- 1 1/4 pounds of ground lamb.

- 1 egg.

- 1 teaspoon of dried oregano.

- 1 teaspoon of dry sherry.

- 1 teaspoon of white wine vinegar.

- 4 minced cloves of garlic.

- Red pepper

- 1/2 cup of chopped green onions.

- 1 tablespoon of chopped mint.

- 2 tablespoons of chopped cilantro.

- 2 tablespoons of dry bread crumbs.

- 1/8 teaspoon of salt to taste.

- 1/4 teaspoon of ground black pepper to taste.

- 5 hamburger buns.

Directions:

1. Preheat a Wood Pellet Smoker or Grill to 350-450 degrees F then grease it grates.

2. Using a large mixing bowl, add in all the ingredients on the list aside from the buns then mix properly to combine with clean hands.

3. Make about five patties out of the mixture then set aside.

4. Place the lamb patties on the preheated grill and cook for about seven to nine minutes turning only once until an inserted thermometer reads 160 degrees F.

5. Serve the lamb burgers on the hamburger, add your favorite toppings and enjoy.

Nutrition:

Calories: 376 Cal

Fat: 18.5 g

Carbohydrates: 25.4 g

Protein: 25.5 g

Fiber: 1.6 g

63. Grilled Lamb Sandwiches
Preparation Time: 5 minutes

Cooking Time: 50 minutes

Servings: 6

Ingredients:

- 1 (4 pounds) boneless lamb.

- 1 cup of raspberry vinegar.

- 2 tablespoons of olive oil.

- 1 tablespoon of chopped fresh thyme.

- 2 pressed garlic cloves.

- 1/4 teaspoon of salt to taste.

- 1/4 teaspoon of ground pepper.

- Sliced bread.

Directions:

1. Using a large mixing bowl, add in the raspberry vinegar, oil, and thyme then mix properly to combine. Add in the lamb, toss to combine then let it sit in the refrigerator for about eight hours or overnight.

2. Next, discard the marinade the season the lamb with salt and pepper to taste. Preheat a Wood Pellet Smoker and grill t0 400-500 degrees F, add in the seasoned lamb and grill for about thirty to forty minutes until it attains a temperature of 150 degrees F.

3. Once cooked, let the lamb cool for a few minutes, slice as desired then serve on the bread with your favorite topping.

Nutrition:

Calories: 407 Cal

Fat: 23 g

Carbohydrates: 26 g

Protein: 72 g

Fiber: 2.3 g

64. Lamb Chops
Preparation Time: 10 minutes

Cooking Time: 12 minutes

Servings: 6

Ingredients:

- 6 (6-ounce) lamb chops

- 3 tablespoons olive oil

- Ground black pepper

Directions:

1. Preheat the pallet grill to 450 degrees F.

2. Coat the lamb chops with oil and then, season with salt and black pepper evenly.

3. Arrange the chops in pallet grill grate and cook for about 4-6 minutes per side.

Nutrition:

Calories: 376 Cal

Fat: 19.5 g

Carbohydrates: 0 g

Protein: 47.8 g

Fiber: 0 g

65. Rosemary Lamb

Preparation Time: 20 Minutes

Cooking Time: 3 Hours & 10 Minutes

Servings: 2 Persons

Ingredients

- One rack lamb, rib
- A bunch of fresh asparagus
- Two rosemary springs
- One dozen baby potato
- 2 tbsp. olive oil
- Pepper & salt to taste
- ½ cup butter

Directions

1. Preheat the grill of your wood pellet to 225 F in advance.
2. Get rid of the membrane from the ribs' backside, after which, drizzle on each side with olive oil; finally sprinkle with the rosemary.
3. Combine the butter with potatoes in a deep baking dish.
4. Place the rack of prepared ribs alongside the dish of potatoes on the grates. Smoke till the inner temperature of the meat displays a 145 degrees F for three hours. During the remaining 15 minutes of cooking, don't neglect to add asparagus to the potatoes & hold to cook until turn tender.
5. Slice the lamb into desired portions & serve with cooked asparagus and potatoes.

Nutrition:

668 Calories

57g Total Fat

665mg Potassium

17g Total Carbohydrates

2.3g Dietary Fiber

0.8g Sugars 22g Protein

66. Smoke Roasted Chicken

Preparation Time: 20 minutes

Cooking Time: 1 hour 20 minutes

Servings: 4-6

Ingredients:

- 8 tablespoon butter, room temperature
- 1 clove garlic, minced
- 1 scallion, minced
- 2 tablespoon fresh herbs such as thyme, rosemary, sage or parsley
- As needed Chicken rub
- Lemon juice
- As needed vegetable oil

Directions:

1. In a small cooking bowl, mix the scallions, garlic, butter, minced fresh herbs, 1-1/2 teaspoon of the rub, and lemon juice. Mix with a spoon.

2.   Remove any giblets from the cavity of the chicken. Wash the chicken inside and out with cold running water. Dry thoroughly with paper towels.

3.   Sprinkle a generous amount of Chicken Rub inside the cavity of the chicken.

4.   Gently loosen the skin around the chicken breast and slide in a few tablespoons of the herb butter under the skin and cover.

5.   Cover the outside with the remaining herb butter.

6.   Insert the chicken wings behind the back. Tie both legs together with a butcher's string.

      Powder the outside of the chicken with more Chicken Rub then insert sprigs of fresh herbs inside the cavity of the chicken.

7.   Set temperature to High and preheat, lid closed for 15 minutes.

8.   Oil the grill with vegetable oil. Move the chicken on the grill grate, breast-side up then close the lid.

9.   After chicken has cooked for 1 hour, lift the lid. If chicken is browning too quickly, cover the breast and legs with aluminum foil.

10.   Close the lid then continue to roast the chicken until an instant-read meat thermometer inserted into the thickest part registers a temperature of 165F

11.   Take off chicken from grill and let rest for 5 minutes. Serve, Enjoy!

Nutrition:

Calories 222kcal

Carbohydrates 11g

Protein 29g

Fat 4g

Cholesterol 62mg

Sodium 616mg

Potassium 620mg

67. Grilled Asian Chicken Burgers

Preparation Time: 5 minutes

Cooking Time: 50 minutes

Servings: 4-6

Ingredients:

- Pound chicken, ground
- 1 cup panko breadcrumbs
- 1 cup parmesan cheese
- 1 small jalapeno, diced
- 2 whole scallions, minced
- 2 garlic clove
- ¼ cup minced cilantro leaves
- 2 tablespoon mayonnaise
- 2 tablespoon chili sauce
- 1 tablespoon soy sauce
- 1 tablespoon ginger, minced
- 2 teaspoon lemon juice

- 2 teaspoon lemon zest

- 1 teaspoon salt

- 1 teaspoon ground black pepper

- 8 hamburger buns

- 1 tomato, sliced

- Arugula, fresh

- 1 red onion sliced

Directions:

1. Align a rimmed baking sheet with aluminum foil then spray with nonstick cooking spray.

2. In a large bowl, combine the chicken, jalapeno, scallion, garlic, cilantro, panko, Parmesan, chili sauce, soy sauce ginger, mayonnaise, lemon juice and zest, and salt and pepper.

3. Work the mixture with your fingers until the ingredients are well combined. If the mixture looks too wet to form patties and add additional more panko.

4. Wash your hands under cold running water, form the meat into 8 patties, each about an inch larger than the buns and about ¾" thick. Use your thumbs or a tablespoon, make a wide, shallow depression in the top of each

5. Put them on the prepared baking sheet. Spray the tops with nonstick cooking spray. If not cooking right away, cover with plastic wrap and refrigerate.

6. Set the Pit Boss grill to 350F then preheat for 15 minutes, lid closed.

7. Order the burgers, depression-side down, on the grill grate. Remove and discard the foil on the baking sheet so you'll have an uncontaminated surface to transfer the slider when cooked.

8. Grill the burgers for about 25 to 30 minutes, turning once, or until they release easily from the grill grate when a clean metal spatula is slipped under them. The internal temperature when read on an instant-read meat thermometer should be 160F.

9. Spread mayonnaise and arrange a tomato slice, if desired, and a few arugula leaves on one-half of each bun. Top with a grilled burger and red onions, if using, then replace the top half of the bun. Serve immediately. Enjoy

Nutrition:

Calories 329kcal

Carbohydrates 10g

Protein 21g

Fat 23g

68. Buffalo Chicken Wings
Preparation Time: 15 Minutes

Cooking Time: 25 Minutes

Servings: 6

Ingredients:

- 2 lb. chicken wings

- 1/2 cup sweet, spicy dry rub

- 2/3 cup buffalo sauce

- Celery, chopped

Directions:

1. Start your wood pellet grill.

2. Set it to 450 degrees F.

3. Sprinkle the chicken wings with the dry rub.

4. Place on the grill rack.

5. Cook for 10 minutes per side.

6. Brush with the buffalo sauce.

7. Grill for another 5 minutes.

8. Dip each wing in the buffalo sauce.

9. Sprinkle the celery on top.

Nutrition:

Calories 935

Total fat 53g

Saturated fat 15g

Protein 107g

Sodium 320mg

69. Sweet and Sour Chicken
Preparation Time: 30 Minutes

Cooking Time: 5 Hours

Servings: 4

Ingredients:

- Eight chicken drumsticks

- 1/4 cup soy sauce

- 1 cup ketchup

- Two tablespoons rice wine vinegar

- Two tablespoons lemon juice

- Two tablespoons honey

- Two tablespoons garlic, minced

- Two tablespoons ginger, minced

- One tablespoon sweet-spicy dry rub

- Three tablespoons brown sugar

Directions:

1. Combine all the sauce fixings in a bowl.

2. Mix well.

3. Take half of the mixture, transfer to another bowl and refrigerate.

4. Add the chicken to the bowl with the remaining sauce.

5. Toss to coat evenly.

6. Cover and refrigerate for 4 hours.

7. When ready to cook, take the chicken out of the refrigerator.

8. Discard the marinade.

9. Turn on your wood pellet grill.

10. Set it to smoke.

11. Set the temperature to 225 degrees F.

12. Smoke the chicken for 3 hours.

13. Serve the chicken with the reserved sauce.

Nutrition:

Calories 935

Total fat 53g

Saturated fat 15g

Protein 107g

Sodium 320mg

70. Buttery Apple Smoked Turkey

Preparation time: 30 minutes

Cooking Time: 6 Hours

Servings: 1

Ingredients:

- Whole Turkey - 1 (10-lbs., 4.5-kgs)
- The Rub
- Minced garlic – 2 tablespoons
- Salt – 2 ½ tablespoons
- The Filling
- Garlic powder – 1 ½ tablespoons
- Black pepper – 1 ½ tablespoons
- Butter – 1 cup
- Unsweetened apple juice – 1 cup
- Fresh apples – 2
- Chopped onion – 1 cup
- The Fire
- Preheat the smoker an hour prior to smoking.
- Use charcoal and hickory wood chips for smoking.

Directions:

1. Preheat a smoker to 225°F (107°C) with charcoal and hickory wood chips.

2. Rub the turkey with salt and minced garlic then set aside.

3. After that, cut the apples into cubes then combine with garlic powder, black pepper, butter, and chopped onion.

4. Pour the unsweetened apple juice over the filling mixture then mix well.

5. Fill the turkey's cavity with the filling mixture then cover the turkey with aluminum foil.

6. Place in the smoker once the smoker is ready and smoke it for 10 hours or until the internal temperature has reached 180°F (82°C). Don't forget to check the smoke and add more wood chips if it is necessary.

7. When the turkey is done, remove from the smoker then let it sit for a few minutes.

8. Unwrap the turkey then place on a flat surface.

9. Cut the turkey into pieces or slices then serve.

10. Enjoy.

Nutrition:

Carbohydrates: 37 g

Protein: 9 g

Sodium: 565 mg

Cholesterol: 49 mg

71. Smoked Turkey Legs grill

Preparation Time: 30 minutes

Cooking Time: 6 Hours

Servings: 1

Ingredients:

- 4 turkey legs
- 2 bay leaves
- 1 cup of BBQ rubs
- 1 tablespoon of crushed allspice berries
- 2 teaspoons of liquid smoke
- ½ gal of cold water
- 4 cups of ice
- 1 gal of warm water
- ½ cup of brown sugar
- ½ cup of curing salt
- 1 tablespoon of peppercorns; whole black

Directions:

1. Take a large stockpot and mix a gallon of warm water to curing salt, rub, peppercorns, brown sugar, liquid smoke, allspice and bay leaves

2. Bring this mix to boil by keeping the flame on high heat and let all salt granules dissolve thoroughly

3. Now let it cool to room temperature

4. Now add ice and cold water and let the whole thing chill in the refrigerator

5. Add turkey legs and make sure they are submerged in the brine

6. Let it stay for a day

7. Now drain the turkey legs and get rid of the brine

8. Wash off the brine from the legs with the help of cold water and then pat it dry

9. Set the grill to preheat by keeping the temperature to 250 degrees F

10. Lay the legs directly on the grate of the grill

11. Smoke it for 4 to 5 hours till the internal temperature reaches 165 degrees F

12. Serve and enjoy

Nutrition:

Carbohydrates: 39 g

Protein: 29 g

Sodium: 15 mg

Cholesterol: 19 mg

72. Smoked Turkey in Beer Brine

Preparation time: 30 minutes

Cooking Time: 6 Hours

Servings: 1

Ingredients:

- Whole Turkey - 1 (10-lbs., 4.5-kgs)

- The Brine

- Water – 1 liter

- Salt – 2 cups

- Brown sugar – 1 sugar

- Bay leaves – 3 leaves

- Thyme – 1 cup

- Chopped onion – 1 cup

- Cold beer – 1 gallon

- The Fire

- Preheat the smoker an hour prior to smoking.

- Use charcoal and hickory wood chips for smoking.

Directions:

1. Pour water into a pot then add salt, brown sugar, bay leaves, thyme, and chopped onion. Bring to boil.

2. Once it is boiled, remove from heat and let it cool. Usually, it will take approximately 30 minutes.

3. When the brine is cool, transfer to a container then pour cold beer into it. Mix until incorporated.

4. Add turkey to the container then refrigerate for 24 hours until the turkey is completely seasoned.

5. After 24 hours, remove from the refrigerator and dry using a paper towel. Set aside.

6. Preheat a smoker to 225°F (107°C) with charcoal and hickory wood chips.

7. Place the turkey in the sm0ker then smoke for 6 hours or until the internal temperature has reached 160°F (71°C).

8. Remove the smoked turkey from the smoker then let it warm.

9. Cut the smoked turkey into pieces or slices then arrange on a serving dish.

10. Serve and enjoy.

Nutrition:

Carbohydrates: 37 g

Protein: 9 g

Sodium: 565 mg

Cholesterol: 49 mg

73. Hot Smoked Turkey with Jelly Glaze

Preparation time: 30 minutes

Cooking Time: 6 Hours

Servings: 1

Ingredients:

- Whole Turkey - 1 (10-lbs., 4.5-kgs)
- The Rub
- Olive oil – ½ cup
- Salt – 3 tablespoons
- Pepper – 2 tablespoons
- The Glaze
- Hot pepper jelly – ¾ cup
- Rice vinegar – 3 tablespoons
- Red pepper flakes – ¼ cup

The Fire

- Preheat the smoker an hour prior to smoking.
- Use charcoal and hickory wood chips for smoking.

Directions:

1. Preheat a smoker to 225°F (107°C) with charcoal and hickory wood chips. Wait until the smoker is ready.

2. Cut the excess fat of the turkey then brush all sides of the turkey with olive oil,

3. Sprinkle salt and pepper over the turkey then place it in the smoker.

4. Smoke the turkey for 6 hours or until the internal temperature has reached 160°F (71°C).

5. Meanwhile, combine hot pepper jelly with rice vinegar and red pepper flakes then mix well.

6. After 6 hours, brush the smoked turkey with the hot pepper jelly mixture then return to the smoker.

7. Smoke for about 20 minutes then remove from the smoker.

8. Let the smoked turkey warm for a few minutes then cut into slices.

9. Arrange on a serving dish then serve.

10. Enjoy!

Nutrition:

Carbohydrates: 27 g

Protein: 19 g

Sodium: 65 mg

Cholesterol: 49 mg

74. Lightly Spiced Smoked Turkey

Preparation time: 30 minutes

Cooking Time: 6 Hours

Servings: 10

Ingredients:

- Whole Turkey - 1 (10-lbs., 4.5-kgs)
- Vegetable oil – ¼ cup
- The Injection
- Beer – ¾ cup, at room temperature
- Butter – ½ cup, melted
- Garlic – 6 cloves
- Worcestershire sauce – 2 ½ tablespoons
- Creole seasoning – 1 ½ tablespoons
- Hot sauce – 1 ½ tablespoons
- Salt – 1 ½ tablespoons
- Cayenne pepper – ½ teaspoon
- The Rub
- Paprika – 1 ½ teaspoons
- Garlic powder – 1 teaspoon
- Onion powder – 1 teaspoon
- Thyme – ¾ teaspoon
- Oregano – ¼ teaspoon
- Cumin – ¼ teaspoon
- Salt – ½ teaspoon
- Black pepper – 1 teaspoon
- The Fire

- Preheat the smoker an hour prior to smoking.

- Use charcoal and hickory wood chips for smoking.

Directions:

1. Preheat a smoker to 225°F (107°C) with charcoal and hickory wood chips. Wait until the smoker is ready.

2. Place garlic, Worcestershire sauce, Creole seasoning, hot sauce, salt, and cayenne pepper in a blender.

3. Pour beer and melted butter into the blender then blend until smooth.

4. Inject all sides of the turkey—give space about 1-inch. Set aside.

5. After that, make the rub by combining paprika with garlic powder, onion powder, thyme, oregano, cumin, salt, and black pepper. Mix well.

6. Rub the turkey with the spice mixture then lightly brush with vegetable oil.

7. When the smoker is ready, place the seasoned turkey in the smoker.

8. Smoke the turkey for 6 hours or until the internal temperature has reached 160°F (71°C).

9. Remove the turkey from the smoker then let it sit for a few minutes.

10. Carve the smoked turkey then serve.

11. Enjoy!

Nutrition:

Carbohydrates: 27 g

Protein: 19 g

Sodium: 65 mg

Cholesterol: 49 mg

75. Grilled Salmon
Preparation Time: 10 minutes

Cooking Time: 4o minutes

Servings: 8

Ingredients:

- 2 pounds salmon (cut into fillets)
- 1/2 cup low sodium soy sauce
- 2 garlic cloves (grated)
- 4 tbsp olive oil
- 2 tbsp honey
- 1 tsp ground black pepper
- ½ tsp smoked paprika
- ½ tsp Italian seasoning
- 2 tbsp chopped green onion

Directions:

1. Incorporate pepper, paprika, Italian seasoning, garlic, soy sauce and olive oil. Add the salmon fillets and toss to combine. Cover the bowl and refrigerate for 1 hour.

2. Remove the fillets from the marinade and let it sit for about 2 hours, or until it is at room temperature.

3. Start the wood pellet on smoke, leaving the lid opened for 5 minutes, or until fire starts.

4. Keep lid unopened and preheat grill to a temperature 350°F for 15 minutes.

5. Do not open lid for 4 minutes or until cooked

6. Flip the fillets and cook for additional 25 minutes or until the fish is flaky.

7. Remove the fillets from heat and let it sit for a few minutes.

8. Serve warm and garnish with chopped green onion.

Nutrition:

Calories: 317 Cal

Fat: 18.8 g

Carbohydrates: 8.3 g

Protein: 30.6 g

Fiber: 0.4 g

76. Barbeque Shrimp
Preparation Time: 20 minutes

Cooking Time: 8 minutes

Servings: 6

Ingredients:

- 2-pound raw shrimp (peeled and deveined)
- ¼ cup extra virgin olive oil
- ½ tsp paprika
- ½ tsp red pepper flakes
- 2 garlic cloves (minced)

- 1 tsp cumin

- 1 lemon (juiced)

- 1 tsp kosher salt

- 1 tbsp chili paste

- Bamboo or wooden skewers (soaked for 30 minutes, at least)

Directions:

1. Combine the pepper flakes, cumin, lemon, salt, chili, paprika, garlic and olive oil. Add the shrimp and toss to combine.

2. Transfer the shrimp and marinade into a zip-lock bag and refrigerate for 4 hours.

3. Let shrimp rest in room temperature after pulling it out from marinade

4. Start your grill on smoke, leaving the lid opened for 5 minutes, or until fire starts. Use hickory wood pellet.

5. Keep lid unopened and preheat the grill to "high" for 15 minutes.

6. Thread shrimps onto skewers and arrange the skewers on the grill grate.

7. Smoke shrimps for 8 minutes, 4 minutes per side.

8. Serve and enjoy.

Nutrition:

Calories: 267 Cal

Fat: 11.6 g

Carbohydrates: 4.9 g

Protein: 34.9 g

Fiber: 0.4 g

77. Pit Boss Grilled Tuna steaks
Preparation Time: 5 minutes

Cooking Time: 4 minutes

Servings: 4

Ingredients:

- 4 (6 ounce each) tuna steaks (1 inch thick)
- 1 lemon (juiced)
- 1 clove garlic (minced)
- 1 tsp chili
- 2 tbsp extra virgin olive oil
- 1 cup white wine
- 3 tbsp brown sugar
- 1 tsp rosemary

Directions:

1. Combine lemon, chili, white wine, sugar, rosemary, olive oil and garlic. Add the tuna steaks and toss to combine.

2. Transfer the tuna and marinade to a zip-lock bag. Refrigerate for 3 hours.

3. Remove the tuna steaks from the marinade and let them rest for about 1 hour

4. Start your grill on smoke, leaving the lid opened for 5 minutes, or until fire starts.

5. Do not open lid to preheat until 15 minutes to the setting "HIGH"

6. Grease the grill grate with oil and place the tuna on the grill grate. Grill tuna steaks for 4 minutes, 2 minutes per side.

7. Remove the tuna from the grill and let them rest for a few minutes.

Nutrition:

Calories: 137 Cal

Fat: 17.8 g

Carbohydrates: 10.2 g

Protein: 51.2 g

Fiber: 0.6 g

78. Oyster in Shells
Preparation Time: 25 minutes

Cooking Time: 8 minutes

Servings: 4

Ingredients:

- 12 medium oysters
- 1 tsp oregano
- 1 lemon (juiced)
- 1 tsp freshly ground black pepper
- 6 tbsp unsalted butter (melted)

- 1 tsp salt or more to taste

- 2 garlic cloves (minced)

- 2 ½ tbsp grated parmesan cheese

- 2 tbsp freshly chopped parsley

Directions:

1. Remove dirt

2. Open the shell completely. Discard the top shell.

3. Gently run the knife under the oyster to loosen the oyster foot from the bottom shell.

4. Repeat step 2 and 3 for the remaining oysters.

5. Combine melted butter, lemon, pepper, salt, garlic and oregano in a mixing bowl.

6. Pour ½ to 1 tsp of the butter mixture on each oyster.

7. Start your wood pellet grill on smoke, leaving the lid opened for 5 minutes, or until fire starts.

8. Keep lid unopened to preheat in the set "HIGH" with lid closed for 15 minutes.

9. Gently arrange the oysters onto the grill grate.

10. Grill oyster for 6 to 8 minutes or until the oyster juice is bubbling and the oyster is plump.

11. Remove oysters from heat. Serve and top with grated parmesan and chopped parsley.

Nutrition:

Calories: 200 Cal

Fat: 19.2 g

Carbohydrates: 3.9 g

Protein: 4.6 g

Fiber: 0.8 g

79. Grilled King Crab Legs
Preparation Time: 10 minutes

Cooking Time: 25 minutes

Servings: 4

Ingredients:

- 4 pounds king crab legs (split)
- 4 tbsp lemon juice
- 2 tbsp garlic powder
- 1 cup butter (melted)
- 2 tsp brown sugar
- 2 tsp paprika
- Black pepper (depends to your liking)

\

Directions:

1. In a mixing bowl, combine the lemon juice, butter, sugar, garlic, paprika and pepper.

2. Arrange the split crab on a baking sheet, split side up.

3. Drizzle ¾ of the butter mixture over the crab legs.

4.   Configure your pellet grill for indirect cooking and preheat it to 225°F, using mesquite wood pellets.

5.   Arrange the crab legs onto the grill grate, shell side down.

6.   Cover the grill and cook 25 minutes.

7.   Remove the crab legs from the grill.

8.   Serve and top with the remaining butter mixture.

Nutrition:

Calories: 480 Cal

Fat: 53.2 g

Carbohydrates: 6.1 g

Protein: 88.6 g

Fiber: 1.2 g

80. Sweet Potato Fries
Preparation Time: 30 Minutes

Cooking Time: 40 Minutes

Servings: 4

Ingredients:

- Three sweet potatoes, sliced into strips

- Four tablespoons olive oil

- Two tablespoons fresh rosemary, chopped

- Salt and pepper to taste

Directions:

1. Set the Pit Boss wood pellet grill to 450 degrees F.

2. Preheat it for 10 minutes.

3. Spread the sweet potato strips in the baking pan.

4. Toss in olive oil and sprinkle with rosemary, salt, and pepper.

5. Cook for 15 minutes.

6. Flip and cook for another 15 minutes.

7. Flip and cook for ten more minutes.

Nutrition:

Calories 118

Total fat 7.6g

Total carbs 10.8g

Protein 5.4g

Sugars 3.7g

Fiber 2.5g,

Sodium 3500mg

Potassium 536mg

81. Potato Fries with Chipotle Peppers
Preparation Time: 30 Minutes

Cooking Time: 30 Minutes

Servings: 4

Ingredients:

- Four potatoes, sliced into strips
- Three tablespoons olive oil
- Salt and pepper to taste
- 1 cup mayonnaise
- Two chipotle peppers in adobo sauce
- Two tablespoons lime juice

Directions:

1. Set the Pit Boss wood pellet grill to high.
2. Preheat it for 15 minutes while the lid is closed.
3. Coat the potato strips with oil.
4. Sprinkle with salt and pepper.
5. Put a baking pan on the grate.
6. Transfer potato strips to the pan.
7. Cook potatoes until crispy.

8. Mix the remaining ingredients.

9. Pulse in a food processor until pureed.

10. Serve potato fries with chipotle dip.

Nutrition:

Calories 118

Total fat 7.6g

Total carbs 10.8g

Protein 5.4g

Sugars 3.7g

Fiber 2.5g,

Sodium 3500mg

Potassium 536mg

82. Pit Boss Grilled Zucchini
Preparation Time: 30 Minutes

Cooking Time: 10 Minutes

Servings: 4

Ingredients:

- Four zucchinis, sliced into strips

- One tablespoon sherry vinegar

- Two tablespoons olive oil

- Salt and pepper to taste

- Two fresh thyme, chopped

Directions:

1. Place the zucchini strips in a bowl.

2. Mix the remaining fixings and pour them into the zucchini.

3. Coat evenly.

4. Set the Pit Boss wood pellet grill to 350 degrees F.

5. Preheat for 15 minutes while the lid is closed.

6. Place the zucchini on the grill.

7. Cook for 3 minutes per side.

Nutrition:

Calories 118

Total fat 7.6g

Total carbs 10.8g

Protein 5.4g

Sugars 3.7g

Fiber 2.5g,

Sodium 3500mg

Potassium 536mg

83. Smoked Potato Salad
Preparation Time: 1 Hour and 15 Minutes

Cooking Time: 40 Minutes

Servings: 4

Ingredients:

- 2 lb. potatoes

- Two tablespoons olive oil

- 2 cups mayonnaise

- One tablespoon white wine vinegar

- One tablespoon dry mustard

- 1/2 onion, chopped

- Two celery stalks, chopped

- Salt and pepper to taste

Directions:

1. Coat the potatoes with oil.

2. Smoke the potatoes in the Pit Boss wood pellet grill at 180 degrees F for 20 minutes.

3. Increase temperature to 450 degrees F and cook for 20 more minutes.

4. Transfer to a bowl and let cool.

5. Peel potatoes.

6. Slice into cubes.

7. Refrigerate for 30 minutes.

8. Stir in the rest of the ingredients.

Nutrition:

Calories 118

Total fat 7.6g

Total carbs 10.8g

Protein 5.4g

Sugars 3.7g

Fiber 2.5g,

Sodium 3500mg

Potassium 536mg

84. Wood Pellet Grilled Zucchini Squash Spears

Preparation Time: 5 minutes,

Cooking Time: 10 minutes.

Servings: 5

Ingredients:

- 4 zucchinis, cleaned and ends cut
- 2 tbsp. olive oil
- 1 tbsp. sherry vinegar
- 2 thyme leaves pulled
- Salt and pepper to taste

Directions:

1. Cut the zucchini into halves then cut each half thirds.
2. Add the rest of the ingredients in a zip lock bag with the zucchini pieces. Toss to mix well.
3. Preheat the wood pellet temperature to 350°F with the lid closed for 15 minutes.
4. Remove the zucchini from the bag and place them on the grill grate with the cut side down.
5. Cook for 4 minutes until the zucchini are tender
6. Remove from grill and serve with thyme leaves. Enjoy.

Nutrition:

Calories: 74

Fat: 5.4g

Carbs: 6.1g

Protein: 2.6g

Sugar: 3.9g

Fiber: 2.3g

Sodium: 302mg

Potassium: 599mg:

85. Grilled French Dip

Preparation Time: 15 Minutes

Cooking Time: 35 Minutes

Servings: 8 to 12

Ingredients:

- 3 lbs. onions, thinly sliced (yellow)
- 2 tbsp. oil
- 2 tbsp. of Butter
- Salt to taste
- Black pepper to taste
- 1 tsp. Thyme, chopped
- 2 tsp. of Lemon juice
- 1 cup Mayo
- 1 cup of Sour cream

Directions:

1. Preheat the grill to high with closed lid.

2. In a pan combine the oil and butter. Place on the grill to melt. Add 2 tsp. salt and add the onions.

3. Stir well and close the lid of the grill. Cook 30 minutes stirring often.

4. Add the thyme. Cook for an additional 3 minutes. Set aside and add black pepper.

5. Once cooled add lemon juice, mayo, and sour cream. Stir to combine. Taste and add more black pepper and salt if needed.

6. Serve with veggies or chips. Enjoy!

Nutrition: Calories: 60 Protein: 4g Carbs: 5g Fat: 6g

86. Roasted Cashews

Preparation Time: 15 Minutes

Cooking Time: 12 Minutes

Servings: 6

Ingredients:

- ¼ cup Rosemary, chopped
- 2 ½ tbsp. Butter, melted
- 2 cups Cashews, raw
- ½ tsp. of Cayenne pepper
- 1 tsp. of salt

Directions:

1. Preheat the grill to 350F with closed lid.

2. In a baking dish layer the nuts. Combine the cayenne, salt rosemary, and butter. Add on top. Toss to combine.

3. Grill for 12 minutes.

4. Serve and enjoy!

Nutrition: Calories: 150 Proteins: 5g Carbs: 7g Fat: 15g

87. Smoked Jerky

Preparation Time: 20 Minutes

Cooking Time: 6 Hours

Servings: 6 to 8

Ingredients:

- 1 Flank Steak (3lb.)
- ½ cup of Brown Sugar
- 1 cup of Bourbon
- ¼ cup Jerky rub
- 2 tbsp. of Worcestershire sauce

- 1 can of Chipotle
- ½ cup Cider Vinegar

Directions:

1. Slice the steak into ¼ inch slices.

2. Combine the remaining ingredients in a bowl. Stir well.

3. Place the steak in a plastic bag and add the marinade sauce. Marinade in the fridge overnight.

4. Preheat the grill to 180F with closed lid.

5. Remove the flank from marinade. Place directly on a rack and on the grill.

6. Smoke for 6 hours.

7. Cover them lightly for 1 hour before serving. Store leftovers in the fridge.

Nutrition: Calories: 105 Protein: 14g Carbs 4g: Fat: 3g

88. Bacon BBQ Bites
Preparation Time: 10 Minutes

Cooking Time: 30 Minutes

Servings: 4

Ingredients:

- 1 tbsp. Fennel, ground
- ½ cup of Brown Sugar
- 1 lb. Slab Bacon, cut into cubes (1 inch)
- 1 tsp. Black pepper
- Salt

Directions:

1. Take an aluminum foil and then fold in half. Once you do that, then turn the edges so that a rim is made. With a fork make small

holes on the bottom. In this way, the excess fat will escape and will make the bites crispy.

2. Preheat the grill to 350F with closed lid.

3. In a bowl combine the black pepper, salt, fennel, and sugar. Stir.

4. Place the pork in the seasoning mixture. Toss to coat. Transfer on the foil.

5. Place the foil on the grill. Bake for 25 minutes, or until crispy and bubbly.

6. Serve and enjoy!

Nutrition: Calories: 300 Protein: 27g Carbs: 4g Fat: 36g

89. Smoked Cheddar Cheese

Preparation Time: 5 minutes

Cooking Time: 5 hour

Servings: 2

Ingredients

2, 8-oz, cheddar cheese blocks

Directions:

1. Preheat and set your Pit Boss grill to 90oF.

2. Place the cheese blocks directly on the grill grate and smoke for about 4 hours.

3. Remove and transfer into a plastic bag, resealable. Refrigerate for about 2 weeks to allow flavor from smoke to permeate your cheese.

4. Now enjoy!

Nutrition:

Calories 115, Total fat 9.5g, Saturated fat 5.4g, Total carbs 0.9g, Net carbs 0.9g, Protein 6.5g, Sugars 0.1g, Fiber 0g, Sodium 185mg, Potassium 79mg

90. Smoked Mac and Cheese

Preparation Time: 2 minutes

Cooking Time: 1 hour

Servings: 2

Ingredients

- 1/2 cup butter, salted

- 1/3 cup flour

- 1/2 tbsp salt

- 6 cups whole milk

- Dash of Worcestershire

- 1/2 tbsp dry mustard

    1 lb small cooked shells, al dente in well-salted water

    2 cups white cheddar, smoked

    2 cups cheddar jack cheese

- 1 cup crushed ritz

Directions:

1. Set your grill on "smoke" and run for about 5-10 minutes with the lid open until fire establishes. Now turn your grill to 325 oF then close the lid.

2. Melt butter in a saucepan, medium, over low--medium heat then whisk in flour.

3. Cook while whisking for about 5-6 minutes over low heat until light tan color.

4. Whisk in salt, milk, Worcestershire, and mustard over low-medium heat stirring frequently until a thickened sauce.

5. Stir noodles, small shells, white sauce, and 1 cup cheddar cheese in a large baking dish, 10x3" high-sided, coated with butter.

6. Top with 1 cup cheddar cheese and ritz.

7. Place on the grill and bake for about 25-30 minutes until a bubbly mixture and cheese melts.

8. Serve immediately. Enjoy!

Nutrition:

Calories 628, Total fat 42g, Saturated fat 24g, Total carbs 38g, Net carbs 37g, Protein 25g, Sugars 11g, Fiber 1g, Sodium 807mg, Potassium 699mg

91. Baked Pulled Pork Stuffed Potatoes
Preparation Time: 10 minutes

Cooking Time: 50 minutes

Servings 6

Ingredients:

- 4 russet potatoes
- Canola oil, as needed
- Salt, to taste
- 2 tablespoons butter, melted
- 3 cups pulled pork
- 1 cup Cheddar cheese
- 1 cup Mozzarella cheese
- 4 tablespoons Pit Boss Sweet & Heat BBQ Sauce

Topping:

- Sour cream
- Chopped bacon
- Chopped green onion

Directions:

1. When ready to cook, set Pit Boss temperature to 450 F (232 C) and preheat, lid closed for 15 minutes.

2. Rub the potatoes with canola oil and sprinkle evenly with salt. Place the potatoes directly on the grill grate and cook for 45 minutes, or until fork tender.

3. Cut the potatoes in half and scoop the flesh out, leaving ¼ inch of the potato on the skin. Brush the inside of the skins with the melted butter and place on a baking tray. Place the tray on the grill and cook for 5 minutes, or until golden brown.

4. In a bowl, stir together the pulled pork, cheeses, and Pit Boss Sweet & Heat BBQ Sauce.

5. Fill the potato skins with the mixture and return to the grill. Cook for 30 seconds, lid closed, or until the cheese is melted.

6. Serve topped with the sour cream, bacon, and green onion.

92. Peanut Butter Cookies
Preparation Time: 5 minutes

Cooking Time: 25 minutes

Servings: 24

Ingredients:

- 1 egg

- 1 cup sugar

- 1 cup peanut butter

Directions:

1. Set your wood pellet grill to smoke.

2. Preheat to high.

3. Mix all the ingredients in one bowl

4. Form cookies from the mixture.

5. Place in a baking pan.

6. Bake in the grill for 20 minutes.

7. Let cool for 5 minutes before serving.

Nutrition:

Calories: 166 Cal

Fat: 8 g

Carbohydrates: 20 g

Protein: 3 g

Fiber: 0 g

93. Pretzels
Preparation Time: 30 minutes

Cooking Time: 1 hour and 30 minutes

Servings: 6

Ingredients:

- 1 packet active instant dry yeast
- 1 tablespoon sugar
- 1 1/2 cups warm water
- 2 oz. melted butter
- 4 ½ cups all-purpose flour
- Cooking spray
- 1/2 cups baking soda
- 10 cups boiling water
- Egg yolks, beaten
- Sea salt

Directions:

1. In a bowl, add the yeast, sugar and warm water.

2. Combine using a mixer.

3. Let sit for 10 minutes.

4.   Once it bubbles, stir in the butter and flour.

5.   Mix for 3 minutes.

6.   Transfer to a bowl.

7.   Spray with oil.

8.   Add a clean towel on top of the bowl.

9.   Let it rise for 1 hour.

10.   Roll the dough into long strips.

11.   Form a knot to create a pretzel shape.

12.   Start your wood pellet grill.

13.   Set it to 350 degrees F.

14.   Add the baking soda to the boiling water.

15.   Drop the pretzels into the boiling water.

16.   Transfer to a baking sheet.

17.   Brush the top with the egg yolk and sprinkle with the salt.

18.   Bake in the wood pellet grill for 20 minutes.

Nutrition:

Calories: 110 Cal

Fat: 1 g

Carbohydrates: 23 g

Protein: 3 g

Fiber: 1 g

Sauces and rubs recipes

94. Classic Kansas City BBQ Sauce
Preparation Time: 10 Minutes

Cooking Time: 15 Minutes

Servings: 24

Ingredients:

- 1/4 cup yellow onion, finely chopped

- 2 tablespoons water

- 2 tablespoons vegetable oil

- 2 cups ketchup

- 1/3 cup brown sugar

- 3 cloves garlic, finely chopped

- 1 tablespoon apple cider vinegar

- 1 tablespoon tomato paste

- 1 tablespoon Worcestershire sauce

- 1 teaspoon liquid hickory smoke

- 1 teaspoon ground mustard

Directions:

1. Place the onion in a food processor and pulse until pureed. Add the water to the onion and pulse few more times.

2. In a medium saucepan, heat the oil and add the onion. When the

onion is just starting to soften, add the remaining ingredients and stir well.

3. Stretch or roll dough to a 12-inch circle.

4. Cook the sauce at a simmer for fifteen minutes, stirring occasionally.

5. Remove the pan from the heat and allow to cool for thirty minutes before using or storing in a mason jar.

Nutrition:

Calories: 799

Sodium: 595mg

Dietary Fiber: 8.6g

Fat: 52.7g

Carbs: 74.9g

Protein: 10g

95. Garlic-Salt Pork Rub

Preparation Time: 5 minutes

Cooking Time: 5 minutes

Servings: 1

Ingredients:

- Eight cloves garlic (minced)
- 1 tbsp. black pepper
- 1 tbsp. paprika
- 1 tbsp. brown sugar

- 1 tbsp. coarse sea salt

Directions:

1. Simply place all ingredients into an airtight jar, stir well to combine then close.
2. Use within six months.

Nutrition:

Calories: 20

Carbs: 5g

Protein: 1g

96. Bill's Best BBQ Sauce
Preparation Time: 10 minutes

Cooking Time: 30 minutes

Servings: 3

Ingredients:

- One small onion, finely chopped
- Two garlic cloves, finely minced
- 2 cups ketchup
- 1 cup of water
- ½ cup molasses
- ½ cup apple cider vinegar
- 5 tbsp. granulated sugar
- 5 tbsps. light brown sugar
- 1 tbsp. Worcestershire sauce
- 1 tbsp. freshly squeezed lemon juice
- 2 tsp. liquid smoke
- 1½ teaspoons freshly ground black pepper
- 1 tbsp. yellow mustard

Directions:

1. On the stove top, place a saucepan over medium heat, combine the onion, garlic, ketchup, water, molasses, apple cider vinegar, granulated sugar, brown sugar, Worcestershire sauce, lemon juice, liquid smoke, black pepper, and mustard. If desired, wait to boil and then reduce the heat to low and simmer for 30 minutes, straining out any bigger chunks.
2. If the sauce is cool completely, then you can transfer to an airtight container and refrigerate for up to 2 weeks, or use a canning process to store for longer.

Nutrition:

Calories: 60

Carbs: 13g

Fat: 1g

Protein: 0g

97. Chimichurri Sauce
Preparation Time: 5 minutes

Cooking Time: 0 minute

Servings: 2

Ingredients:

- ½ cup extra-virgin olive oil
- One bunch of fresh parsley stems removed
- One bunch of fresh cilantro stems removed
- One small red onion, chopped
- 3 tbsp. dried oregano
- 1 tbsp. minced garlic
- Juice of 1 lemon
- 2 tbsp. red wine vinegar
- 1 tsp. salt

- 1 tsp. freshly ground black pepper
- 1 tsp. cayenne pepper

Directions:

1. Using a blender or processor, combine all of the ingredients and pulse several times until finely chopped.
2. The chimichurri sauce will keep in an airtight container in the refrigerator for up to 5 days.

Nutrition:

Calories: 51

Carbs: 1g

Fat: 5g

Protein: 1g

98. Chipotle Butter

Preparation Time: 10 minutes

Cooking Time: 5 minutes

Servings: 1

Ingredients:

- 1 cup (2 sticks) salted butter
- Two chipotle chilies in adobo sauce, finely chopped
- 2 tsp. adobo sauce
- 2 tsp. salt
- Juice of 1 lime

Directions:

1. On the stovetop, in a small saucepan over medium heat, melt the butter. Stir in the chopped chilies, adobo sauce, salt, and lime juice, continuing to stir until the salt is dissolved, about 5 minutes. Remove from the heat.

2. Serve the chipotle butter hot or cold. It will give shelf life in an airtight container in the refrigerator for up to 2 weeks.

Nutrition:

Calories: 60

Carbs: 1g

Fat: 6g

Protein: 0g

Dessert recipes

99. Classic Kansas City BBQ Sauce

Preparation Time: 10 Minutes

Cooking Time: 15 Minutes

Servings: 24

Ingredients:

- 1/4 cup yellow onion, finely chopped
- 2 tablespoons water
- 2 tablespoons vegetable oil
- 2 cups ketchup
- 1/3 cup brown sugar
- 3 cloves garlic, finely chopped
- 1 tablespoon apple cider vinegar
- 1 tablespoon tomato paste
- 1 tablespoon Worcestershire sauce
- 1 teaspoon liquid hickory smoke
- 1 teaspoon ground mustard

Directions:

6. Place the onion in a food processor and pulse until pureed. Add the water to the onion and pulse few more times.

7. In a medium saucepan, heat the oil and add the onion. When the onion is just starting to soften,

add the remaining ingredients and stir well.

8. Stretch or roll dough to a 12-inch circle.

9. Cook the sauce at a simmer for fifteen minutes, stirring occasionally.

10. Remove the pan from the heat and allow to cool for thirty minutes before using or storing in a mason jar.

Nutrition:

Calories: 799

Sodium: 595mg

Dietary Fiber: 8.6g

Fat: 52.7g

Carbs: 74.9g

Protein: 10g

100. Garlic-Salt Pork Rub

Preparation Time: 5 minutes

Cooking Time: 5 minutes

Servings: 1

Ingredients:

- Eight cloves garlic (minced)
- 1 tbsp. black pepper
- 1 tbsp. paprika
- 1 tbsp. brown sugar
- 1 tbsp. coarse sea salt

Directions:

3. Simply place all ingredients into an airtight jar, stir well to combine then close.
4. Use within six months.

Nutrition:

Calories: 20

Carbs: 5g

Protein: 1g

101. Bill's Best BBQ Sauce
Preparation Time: 10 minutes

Cooking Time: 30 minutes

Servings: 3

Ingredients:

- One small onion, finely chopped
- Two garlic cloves, finely minced
- 2 cups ketchup
- 1 cup of water
- ½ cup molasses
- ½ cup apple cider vinegar
- 5 tbsp. granulated sugar
- 5 tbsps. light brown sugar
- 1 tbsp. Worcestershire sauce
- 1 tbsp. freshly squeezed lemon juice
- 2 tsp. liquid smoke
- 1½ teaspoons freshly ground black pepper
- 1 tbsp. yellow mustard

Directions:

3. On the stove top, place a saucepan over medium heat, combine the onion, garlic, ketchup, water, molasses, apple cider vinegar, granulated sugar, brown sugar, Worcestershire sauce, lemon juice, liquid smoke, black pepper, and mustard. If desired, wait to boil and then reduce the heat to low and simmer for 30 minutes, straining out any bigger chunks.
4. If the sauce is cool completely, then you can transfer to an airtight container and refrigerate for up to 2 weeks, or use a canning process to store for longer.

Nutrition:

Calories: 60

Carbs: 13g

Fat: 1g

Protein: 0g

102. Chimichurri Sauce
Preparation Time: 5 minutes

Cooking Time: 0 minute

Servings: 2

Ingredients:

- ½ cup extra-virgin olive oil
- One bunch of fresh parsley stems removed
- One bunch of fresh cilantro stems removed
- One small red onion, chopped
- 3 tbsp. dried oregano
- 1 tbsp. minced garlic
- Juice of 1 lemon
- 2 tbsp. red wine vinegar
- 1 tsp. salt
- 1 tsp. freshly ground black pepper
- 1 tsp. cayenne pepper

Directions:

3. Using a blender or processor, combine all of the ingredients and pulse several times until finely chopped.
4. The chimichurri sauce will keep in an airtight container in the refrigerator for up to 5 days.

Nutrition:

Calories: 51

Carbs: 1g

Fat: 5g

Protein: 1g

103. Chipotle Butter

Preparation Time: 10 minutes

Cooking Time: 5 minutes

Servings: 1

Ingredients:

- 1 cup (2 sticks) salted butter
- Two chipotle chilies in adobo sauce, finely chopped
- 2 tsp. adobo sauce
- 2 tsp. salt
- Juice of 1 lime

Directions:

3. On the stovetop, in a small saucepan over medium heat, melt the butter. Stir in the chopped chilies, adobo sauce, salt, and lime juice, continuing to stir until the salt is dissolved, about 5 minutes. Remove from the heat.
4. Serve the chipotle butter hot or cold. It will give shelf life in an airtight container in the refrigerator for up to 2 weeks.

Nutrition:

Calories: 60

Carbs: 1g

Fat: 6g

Protein: 0g

Conclusion

The Pit boss pellet grill has made grilling simpler and safer for humanity, and grilling, which is part of "dietetic" cooking, has been made easier by the Pit boss grill. Providing us with the delicious meal we have been missing and thereby enhancing our quality of life. This book contains a variety of recipes that you can cook at home using your new Pit boss Pellet grill. The tenderness and tasty BBQ in the recipes can provide a lot of satisfaction.

The Pit boss barbecues are electric, and they are regulated by a standard 3-position mechanism. A cylindrical unit, like a pellet stove, transports pellets from the storage to the fireplace. The Pit boss Grill smoker ensures that your meat and other recipes work out perfectly. This smoker creates a wonderful atmosphere for your food. To achieve such a genuine flavor, high-quality materials and precise smoking are needed. It is best if you can reach the highest degree of smoking accuracy possible so that your meat and other recipes work out perfectly. Furthermore, if you want to add more spice to your recipes, use the best wood pellet for cooking.

Many people ask me why I choose Pit boss pellet grills, and you would think, well, the answer is easy and straightforward, and yes! It is right in front of us. What is the explanation for this?

It cooks over a wood fire, resulting in exceptional flavor because nothing compares real wood, real smoking, and natural aroma. The cooking method has evolved significantly. Expert chefs are known for experimenting with different flavors and ingredients to produce a delectable and tasty dish.

Grilling is one of the most common cooking methods for achieving a perfect flavor in your dishes. Grilling is a better cooking method than others because it benefits the food, retains flavor, and preserves nutrients. A Pit boss grill smoker's wood pellet grill, on the other hand, helps you to grill your food easily and with less effort and smoke. The benefit of having a Pit boss grill smoker in your home is that it is flexible, helps you cook food faster, offers a temperature control scale, and is one of the most critical aspects of cooking.

It is a flexible grill. In fact, the Pit boss grill smoker can be used to grill, smoke, bake, roast, and stew everything you can think of. This Pit boss grill smoker is a powerful tool that offers excellent service.

As we can all attest, Pit boss has made using the pellet grill simple: its intuitive control panel has a power button and a knob that allows you to easily change the temperature.

Finally, we should add that we can always find new flavors in our dishes through grilling: you can smoke your dishes with Pit boss pellets, giving them a constantly new and different taste. The Pit boss Grill smoker is the answer to your taste buds' prayers. Do not waste any more time; get your own smoker and begin cooking your favorite recipes with this book.

9 781802 892253